Collecting
Carlton Ware

David Serpell

Francis Joseph

Acknowledgements

Particular thanks and acknowledgements are extended to:

Kathy Niblett and Miranda Goodby, Potteries Museum and Art Gallery, Stoke-on-Trent

Ruth Dennison, Celia and David, Coalport China Museum, Ironbridge Gorge, Telford.

Hamish Wood, Gladstone Working Pottery Museum, Hanley.

Roger and Rosemary Biggs, Hemel Hempstead.

Beverley, 30, Church Street, London. 0171 262 1576

Beth Adams, Alfie's Antique Centre, Church Street, London 0467 783956

Eddie Page, of Goss Cottage, Sheringham. 01263 824094

Dennis Harwood, Much Ado About Deco, Stratford-on-Avon 01789 204180

© Francis Joseph Publications 1999
ISBN 1 870703 43 X
Second edition

Published in the UK by
Francis Joseph Publications
5 Southbrook Mews, London SE12 8LG
Tel: 0181 318 9580
e-mail: info@carltonware.co.uk

Typeset by
E J Folkard Print Services
199 Station Road, Crayford, Kent DA1 3QF

Printed by
Greenwich Press
Standard House, Eastmoor Sreet, London SE7

Contents

The Author

David Serpell lives and writes in Suffolk, though his interests take him all over the British Isles. In addition to being keen collectors of Carlton Ware and early plastics, he and his wife share a fascination with the style and artefacts of the 1930's, and a keen interest in mediaeval and twentieth century history. An enthusiastic walker and birdwatcher, David is also a well known writer on touring caravans.

Authors Note

My thanks are due to many, many people who have helped me in small or great measure with the preparation of this book. Dealers and collectors, friends and family have all given their time and endured my questions, each answer contributing a further piece to the varied tapestry of the Carlton story. This book does not pretend to be exhaustive - indeed, if it were it would have to be many times the size, and would no longer be a Handbook. By the same token, while I have endeavoured to learn my lessons well, there may well be errors contained within. For any such errors I make full apology here, and accept the blame – to all those who have helped so much can only go my warmest thanks. My gratitude is offered particularly to a small group of people, listed on page 2, who have helped me by making available specific material for certain chapters, or who have allowed their prized possessions to be photographed.

Above all I am indebted to my wife Sharon, without whose sharp eyes I would have missed some fascinating items, and who is both my greatest supporter and my sternest critic; and to our good friends Beverley and Beth Adams for their great fund of experience and knowledge, and their good humoured help and encouragement.

Key to back cover

*From back left: pattern 4018 **Secretary Bird** beneath tree with exotic foliage on dark red ground, large vase (£2588); pattern 3405 the **Floral Comets** pattern on a large wall plaque (£3176); pattern 3814 the **Wagon Wheels** design on mottled dark red large vase (£3293); pattern 3361 **Jazz** pattern against a dark blue on a large bulbous vase lustre ground (£4705); pattern 3015 the famous **Chinaland** pattern on a mottled red ground, on a medium ginger jar (£2000); pattern 3352 on a medium bulbous vase showing **Jazz** on dark red (£2235); pattern 3387 **Floral Comets** on an olive green background, small to medium ginger jar (£329); pattern 3651 a pedestal powder bowl in **Scimitar** design, small to medium powder bowl (£882); pattern 3767, sought after **Mephistopheles** figure dressed in red on a pale blue ground medium jug (£2000); and pattern 3721 superb geometric design known as **Rainbow Fan**, medium vase (£2352). Courtesy Christies Prices realised in August 1998.*

Foreword
Francis J Salmon

As a publisher of books on Twentieth-Century English Ceramics, it will come as no surprise to you that Carlton Ware has long been regarded as an important subject for me. I published the first edition in 1994 in order to meet the inherent demand for information regarding this subject. Hitherto, there had been nothing for collectors but empty promises that someone, somewhere was going to come up with something. Consequently, I did what I could, enlisting the help of friends, in particular Pat and Howard Watson, Beverley and Beth, and Dennis Harwood. Howard Watson was particularly nostalgic for the then redundant Carlton Ware name, and I wondered, just wondered, whether it was purchasable. I could not buy it at the time, but in 1997 I called John McCluskey of Grosvenor Ceramics, the owner of the trade name and other assets, and secured a purchase. I inherited an Aladdin's Cave of moulds dating back to goodness knows when, along with the trade name and goodwill of the company, but I did not even suspect, at that time, how exiting things were to become.

My experience as co-owner of Kevin Francis, still making collectable toby jugs and other figures, had taught me a great deal about the pottery industry. As the recession bit hard in the early nineties, I sold my interest in the company, and four years later I was ready to enter the world of ceramic production once more. The support of so many friends and contacts within the business was a real boon to me. Among them, Roger Bairstow at the Bairstow Manor Pottery in Stoke-on-Trent was especially helpful and he is now producing all the Carlton Ware for us. He and his wife, Brenda have worked extremely hard to uncover the many moulds that were delivered upon purchase, and they also managed to rescue some moulds from potters who had acquired them from the 1989 sale of assets. Among them was a delightful series of Carlton Children dressed as adults – a wartime series that had never been put into production and dubbed by Roger the *Carlton Kids*. The excitement of checking the mould numbers against the records we had was immense – they could easily have been lost for all time. Also among these moulds were a series of small figures (a Negro Band and a set of Pixies come immediately to mind) and even today we have not been through all the moulds we inherited. It is always delightful to see the latest slip cast assembly of moulds form a new figure or ornament.

Our policy from the very beginning has been to introduce new items relating to the 1990s, and not to reproduce or imitate the wares of the 1930s. Where there is a useable mould, like the classic teapot design of the Red Baron, we are producing it with new colours, in varying guises and with clear labels and boxes that indicate the modernity of the items. Our backstamp includes the TM mark that is commonplace nowadays and should indicate to anyone uncertain that the piece they have is post 1997.

The inspiration for the figurines we have introduced is the clear association between Carlton Ware and flowers – so many designs are based on flowers, whether lithograph or relief moulded that we decided upon a series of Carlton Girls that embody the spirit of Carlton Ware. The first to take my eye was the lithographed and enamelled 'Hollyhocks' pattern, and Douglas V Tootle did an excellent three dimensional interpretation of a nude figure nestled in the flowers. The result was lovely, and the new series was born.

Another inspiration was the figure of Mephistopheles – or The Red Devil. He appears in rare examples of superb lustre wares – often with Tiger's Eye trees in the background. A bowl with the Red Devil in place appeared at Christies in 1997 and fetched an enormous £4700! He is therefore the inspiration for the first in a Character Series of where each piece is limited to just 500. Following on from him are other characters from the 1930s – the Jester, Masquerade, Harlequin and so on.

There are other plans in the pipeline too numerous to mention. Suffice to say that Carlton Ware is very much back in production. Quality and Good Humour seem to me to be the bywords for this fabulous company – and I promise to uphold them.

Finally I would like to thank David Serpell for his wonderful efforts in researching this book. This second edition is the kind of book that collectors of Carlton Ware have been wanting – full of information and photographs of over a century of Carlton Ware. He has done a fantastic job with real dedication, helped, no doubt, by his wife, Sharon. Without them this book would not have been possible and without the inspiration of Pat and Howard Watson, the great name of Carlton Ware would only be of historical importance today.

Introduction

Something for everyone

Varied, valuable, decorative and fun – Carlton Ware is all of these; but most of all it is true to say that today Carlton Ware of every era, and in every one of its many styles is *collectable*.

Collectability is rather a hard condition to define. To become collectable items must have appeal to a wide range of people – and this appeal will be made up of a combination of properties. Quality in manufacture, investment value, eye appeal, curiosity, diversity and affordability – all of these play their part in deciding which items arrive on the scene, last a few years and are then forgotten; and which have that lasting appeal which makes them sought after 'objects of desire' for succeeding generations.

Of course in pottery, as in most walks of life, 'one man's meat is another man's poison'. So it is even within Carlton – but the output of the factory at Copeland Street, Stoke-on-Trent for almost a century displayed such range, such consistent high quality, and such imagination that Carlton Ware holds a unique place in many collectors' hearts and minds. Whether individual fancy takes you into Victoriana or table ware, exotic lustre items or Heraldic china, witty novelties or dainty patterns of fruits and berries, such is the breadth of their range that collecting Carlton truly offers something for everyone, whether on a budget, or as serious investor.

From the simple to the luxurious, from plain styles to the highly decorated, Carlton Ware has already celebrated over a hundred years of existence. There were fears that there would be no more Carlton in the early 1990s after the closure of the original factory – but such thoughts were premature. A new owner acquired the famous marque in 1997, and entirely new Carlton Ware figures, with all the hallmarks of quality, individuality and style, and bearing the famous scriptmark are beginning to appear. Some of these are entirely new designs, while a small number are original 1940s designs, now in production for the first time. There can be little doubt that these will quickly become as sought after and valued as all the previous century of Carlton Ware richness and variety.

The quality of Carlton Ware

The uninitiated sometimes ask collectors: *"Why Carlton Ware – what's so special about it?"*, and, of course, there is no single answer which defines all of Carlton's appeal. As we will see later in this book, the Copeland Street works produced a simply staggering variety of wares over some 99 years, but throughout most of this period one word provides a key to Carlton's continuing success over such a long period – and to its enduring popularity with collectors from many walks of life today. That word is Quality.

Even in their earliest years when the young company's Blush Ware had to gain acceptance against established names like Crown Devon, they succeeded by placing an emphasis on the highest standards, both in manufacture and in decoration. Clear, fine mouldings (although better were to come) and delicate handpainted floral decorations were the order of the day. When Wiltshaw and Robinson began to introduce product ideas of their own in the period leading up to the First World War, quality was again a hallmark. Production included many matt black items, with both transfer and enamel designs, among them the interesting 'cloisonné' ware, imitating cloisonné jewellery. During this period they also introduced hand enamelled parian Crested china and Commemorative Ware for a completely different market, very successfully penetrating a market established over twenty years by W. H. Goss. Once more the fineness of their castings and the superb detail of their hand enamelled crests offered quality to a ready public.

"Technique which is exceptional"
However it was between the wars that the range and diversity of Carlton Ware reached its peak. Their mouldings of this period are so often just a bit finer in the hand, more elegant to the eye than any other British factory of the day, even before we consider the range of luxurious lustre finishes, the sumptuous designs and dazzling colours, both under and over glaze. Carlton without doubt developed some of the most sophisticated techniques for lithographic transfer printing of any factory, and these alone give great colour and interest to many designs. On top of these were applied a range of complex lustre finishes, often incorporating oxides and salts of precious metals, and these succeeded in imparting a clarity and three dimensional depth to their pieces that very few could match.

The final jewel in their crown was a superb team of paintresses, whose deft precision in applying the over glaze enamels in an amazing array of colours provided the finishing touches to make Carlton Ware designs so eye catching and desirable. From among the British factories only Crown Devon could be said to come close, and this was achieved to some extent by sharing the workforce of paintresses. However, by this time the Fieldings factory had lost its pre-eminence in creating fine and distinctive pottery shapes. It is often possible to tell Crown Devon of this period from Carlton Ware as you pick it up by the somewhat heavier, coarser feel, regardless of decoration.

These lustre pieces coexisted with the delightful floral embossed ranges, such as **Rock Garden** and **Buttercup**, **Blackberry** and **Wild Rose**. Other factories produced moulded items, but once again the fine detail in the moulding of their leaves, berries and flowers, along with careful hand painting made Carlton Ware items big sellers then – and highly desirable now. The same care was applied even in the production of items of lesser value such as cruets, napkin rings, figurines and advertising figures, with the result that all of these are today rightly considered attractive and highly collectable.

In reflecting on the insistence on quality which was so characteristic of Carlton at this time the unique, frosted glaze achieved on the beautiful Glacielle animal figures cannot be overlooked. In October 1938 *The Pottery Gazette and Glass Trade Review* described this range as embodying 'technique, from the modelling down to the last finishing touch' which is 'exceptional'. Such praise can, perhaps, be reiterated about much of Carlton's output during the 1920s and 1930s.

Clean curves and simple colours
When styles and popular tastes changed after the Second World War Carlton Ware's new designs showed clean, sweeping curves and simple colours. Despite the changes in style, the quality of their moulding remained excellent, and both the embossed patterns like **Poppy**, **Grape**, **Convolvulus** and **Magnolia**, and the post-war lustre wares are rightly enjoyed by collectors today. Both before and after the War the factory made many novelty items, including an extraordinary range of cruets. These too are to a standard that makes them sought after, both by contemporary Carlton collectors, and by those with a special interest in cruets.

The quality of Carlton's novelty wares was sustained during the 1970s making them fun rather than clumsy, with the Walking Ware range enjoying a great vogue (and indeed it is still in limited production by the Price Kensington factory who bought the moulds in 1992).

The 1990s – Grosvenor Ceramics and Francis Joseph
Between 1989 and 1992 the new owner of the Carlton Ware name, Grosvenor Ceramics, produced limited quantities of Carlton Ware, using familiar moulds from both novelty and lustre ranges. These items are of interest in their own right, though it has to be said that neither the quantity nor the quality of hand painting is on par with earlier years. They are, of course, normally in pristine condition, and while the decoration is limited they offer a route to ownership of lustreware at much lower prices than the earlier production.

In 1997, however, the highest standards were re-established when new series of figures started to appear after the acquisition of the Carlton Ware name by Francis Joseph. These are of delightful freshness and quality, and already bid for the enthusiasm of collectors in the twenty-first century.

1890 to 1998 – the Carlton Ware story

Early Days
When J. F. Wiltshaw formed a partnership with the brothers J. A. and W. H. Robinson in 1890 he cannot have foreseen that the company they founded would last, with changes, for more than a hundred years. That company, Wiltshaw and Robinson, was entering an already crowded market place. Towards the end of the Victorian era there were a number of well established pottery manufacturers, with several producing the Vellum or Blush Ware which was popular at the time in many reasonably well-to-do households. In particular one, Fielding's Crown Devon, held a pre-eminent position in the market place, with a wide range of jugs and bowls, comports and plates made to a high standard, and beautifully decorated. It is a tribute both to the energy of James Frederick Wiltshaw and his partners, and to their emphasis on high standards in manufacture right from the start that they were able to establish the young company's product.

The Edwardian period – souvenirs and sobriety
While they could not expect immediately to overtake the market leader, they clearly made high quality a watchword in the new company – and so it was to stay. At the turn of the century they branched out into Commemorative, or Crested Ware made in parian, a variety of china, again against established competition like Goss, Shelley and Arcadia, and within a very few years had achieved a wide customer base for a quality article. During the same period Blush Ware was progressively replaced with matt black wares, initially with floral decoration in peonies and prunus blossom; and the interesting 'cloisonné ware' where enamel pictures of flowers and birds were outlined in bold bands of gilt to resemble the cloisonné type of jewellery.

1911 – a parting of the ways
However there were disagreements between the directors, and these came to a head amongst ill feeling in 1911, when J. F. Wiltshaw parted company from the Robinson brothers, and the direction of the firm passed entirely to the Wiltshaw family. James Frederick was joined just before the war by his son, F. C. (Cuthbert) Wiltshaw, who almost immediately joined up and went away to become a fighter ace in the conflict – and survived. In 1918 he returned, only to lose his father in a tragic accident when he slipped trying to board a moving train. For the next 48 years Cuthbert was to lead the company through some of its greatest days.

Between the wars – the Deco Age
It is arguably the period between the two World Wars that saw Wiltshaw and Robinson at its peak. Like his father Cuthbert was clearly a man of immense drive and imagination, for under him Carlton Ware achieved new heights. Matt black finishes were teamed with completely new decorations reflecting public interest in the 'mysterious orient', and gained attractive green, ivory or terracotta friezes. The factory became expert in production of up to a dozen superb lustre finishes for their finer wares. Following the Paris Exhibition of Decorative Arts in 1925, Wiltshaw and Robinson welcomed the dawn of the Art Deco period with bold and colourful stylised designs which dazzled the eye in

a wide range of colours and shapes. The combination of craftsmanship, technique and artistry which gave rise to such stunning designs as **Egyptian Fan**, *Bell* and *Babylon* have never been equalled, and the succession of fabulous birds, including **Paradise Bird and Tree**, *Crested Bird and Water Lily* and the stunning *Secretary Bird* are also among some of the most striking patterns ever devised. Production blossomed at the Copeland Street Works during the 1920s and 1930s to include more mundane items beside the up-market lustre pieces.

1929 – Handcraft and Oven-to-Table Wares

In the late 1920s Carlton's range had expanded to include table ware, such as the pretty, pearlised Orange Ware; and in 1929 Carlton were the very first to market Oven-to-Table Ware. In that same year the first of the Handcraft designs appeared, with matt glazes, and softer, more folksy designs, often of stylised flowers or landscapes. These struck a quieter note, and also were considerably cheaper than the highly decorated lustre items, some of which required eight or nine separate operations to complete them. With all this going on in 1928 the company acquired the firm of Birks, Rawlins & Co, both to assist with expansion into bone china, and to use as a decorating factory. Unfortunately this was not a success as Birks, Rawlins carried high costs, and the extra factory was closed in 1933. Around this time, in 1932/3 the first of the acclaimed floral embossed ranges made their appearance, and these quickly multiplied in number and popularity, lasting up to and after the Second World War.

Post-War technical innovations

Clearly Cuthbert Wiltshaw and his staff had been planning future developments with care during the war years when austerity had kept investment severely restricted. In 1946, however, the company installed an entirely new electric Glost (or glaze firing) oven, and this was followed a couple of years later by a new electric Biscuit (or first firing) oven. These represented a massive step forward in production technology, as they were tunnel ovens which offered the potential for continuous production. Trolleys loaded with product ran on rails through the ovens, being warmed progressively up to firing temperatures, and then slowly cooled down again before emerging for the next stage. The old system where everything had to be packed by size into Saggars and loaded in huge batches into bottle kilns was virtually swept away, replaced by cheaper, faster production where small groups of various items intended for a particular market or customer could be kept together through several stages of the process.

With the new methods came new designs, introduced alongside the post-war versions of established favourites. In the 1940s the latest lustre wares were produced in the Royale range of colours, Rouge, Bleu, Noire and Vert (Red, Blue, Black and Green). Apart from Black, these were distinguished from the earlier hues of the 1930s by their homogeneity and uniformity, where the earlier colours tended to be mottled, or have a certain amount of visual texture. Vert Royale was a sharper, slightly more acidic shade than earlier greens, while two blues appeared – Bleu Royale, a quite pale blue, often shaded to black at the edges, and a new navy blue, darker and smoother than the earlier powder coat blues. Hand painted designs including **Spider's Web**, *Bullrushes* and **New Stork** were very popular, alongside the latest incarnation of the evergreen chinoiserie patterns like **New Mikado**.

Fruit and floral embossed designs continued, with some new, bolder and somewhat less dainty designs appearing, including **Poppy, Daisy, Hydrangea, Vine and Grape**.

1950s – In tune with post-war styles

When rationing and restrictions came to an end in the early 1950s, and production of decorative wares was permitted again, the Copeland Street Works quickly entered another new phase. The company emphasised that it was back in the business of producing decorative pottery by incorporating the word 'Handpainted' into its backstamp for almost all items (whether they were or not!), and entered into the post-war era with enthusiasm. Fine lustre wares, notably the Royale ranges continued the tradition at the top of the market, while new asymmetric designs with swept curves and clean lines such as the **Windswept, Leaf** and **Pinstripe** ranges which were in keeping with the tastes of the day progressively replaced the earlier fruits and berries. Quality, however continued to be high, and today the twin coloured leaves, **Pinstripe** designs and late 1950s embossed designs like **Convolvulus** and **Magnolia** are popular all over again. In 1958, perhaps a little overdue, the company changed its name to Carlton Ware Ltd., just as the new **Windswept, Magnolia** and **Pinstripe** ranges were being launched.

The late 1960s – recession hits the industry

The 1960s saw recession bite, and Cuthbert Wiltshaw, now an old man, passed away in 1966. He left a widow and four daughters but no sons to take over the business. In 1967 Carlton Ware Ltd. as it was now called, was sold to Arthur Wood and Son (Longport) plc. Anthony Wood, the son of Arthur, became Managing Director of Carlton Ware Ltd. at the beginning of what was to be a troubled period. Manufacturing and distributive costs were affected by conflict with the Arab oil producers during the 1970s, and the whole of the UK economy was suffering from the after effects of the 'Flower Power' days of the late 1960s when too many people convinced themselves that the world owed them a living without much work. This coincided with an excess of Trade Union influence along similar lines, and so severe recession along with devaluation resulted.

1970s – Walking Ware to the rescue

In this difficult atmosphere there was still room for individual brilliance to shine. At the beginning of the 1970s a married couple, Roger Michell and Danka Napiorkowska, were recruited to Carlton Ware Ltd. to develop their own designs, particularly the famous Walking Ware. Roger and Danka had a small studio pottery 'Lustre Pottery', where they had developed the initial Walking Ware designs to be featured in an exhibition in London. The range made a big public impact, with the public and the press being full of praise for this novel idea with its cuteness and originality. The couple were inundated with potential orders, but their Lustre Pottery was quite unable to cope with the required volume of production. After negotiation agreement was reached with Anthony Wood, and the early success of Walking Ware led to a contract in 1973 for Roger and Danka to design exclusively for Carlton. This arrangement was to last for about eight years.

The success of Walking Ware may well have saved the company during the 1970s. The idea gave birth to numerous variations, such as the Caribbean range, the Running, Jumping and Standing Still range, and the Circus range; as well as individual novelty items including a Silver Jubilee mug, a Santa Claus mug and St. Valentines Day items. Although Arthur Wood produced other items from the Carlton Ware repertoire, and indeed tried reintroducing some earlier successes such as **Apple Blossom** in the late 1970s, nothing else took off in the same way as the Michell/Napiorkowska designs.

1989 – the end of Copeland Street Works
Despite the success of the designs of Roger and Danka, Carlton Ware Ltd. was in real trouble as the severe recession of the early 1980s took hold. Production declined, and eventually in 1987 the company was sold by the Wood Group to County Potteries plc, a holding company which had already purchased James Kent Ltd at Fenton, and had the stated intention of acquiring other potteries with the object of rejuvenating the ailing industry around Stoke-on-Trent. Whether this stated intention was genuine or not it was never to see fruition. In 1988 County Potteries announced the closure of the Copeland Street Works, and a merger with James Kent. There was a short production run under the name of Carlton Ware from Fenton in 1988, during which the Hovis range first produced in the 1970s was revived, but despite the announcement of the merger in February 1989 this never became an active reality. With mounting debts the Receivers were called in early in 1989, and the famous Copeland Street factory was sold to a firm of developers as an empty shell in April of the same year.

Grosvenor Ceramics – 1989 to 1997
In May 1989 John McCluskey, owner of Grosvenor Ceramics, a company specialising in the manufacture of ceramic door knobs, purchased the name, pattern and shape books, goodwill and some moulds from the receivers. After transfer to his factory at Stone, south of Stoke, he produced a centenary vase in 1990, accompanied by the re-issue of a number of familiar Carlton shapes in two lustre ranges. Top of the range featured repeats of earlier Chinoiserie and bird designs, though with greatly reduced amounts of handpainted pattern. A second range, called **Moonlight** featured underglaze transfer printed Irises. In addition he produced a large range of novelty teapots. Like the lustre items, these can normally be easily distinguished from earlier Copeland Street items.

Francis Joseph – Carlton Ware 1997 to . . .
Production at Grosvenor did not take off as hoped, and ceased in 1992. For five years the Carlton name lay dormant, until purchased by Francis Joseph in early 1997. In amongst the collection of moulds and half made pieces which Francis Joseph acquired from Grosvenor Ceramics were discovered a small group of original Plaster of Paris moulds for a group of previously unknown, nursery style figures, some in Forces uniforms. Careful research revealed that these little figures were modelled around 1940, as part of a set of figures, some adult in style, and some modelled as kids, which included a Barrage Balloon and a Warship, as well as a Nurse, a Bridal Pair, a Sailor and an Airman. This set probably never went into production because of wartime restrictions on handpainted articles. Of a total of thirteen figures originally designed only a handful of the 1940 moulds have survived; but these pieces are now being produced, and form the basis for a whole new series. Many new designs are now being put into production and with the launch of the new Carlton Ware Collectors Club there is an air of excitement among collectors once more.

Infinite variety – Carlton's diversity

Buy Carlton – first with the latest and best went the slogan used for many years in Wiltshaw and Robinson's advertising. With hindsight perhaps their claim was not too far from the truth. Carlton Ware products have always moved with the times, reflecting closely the public taste in each period – and in a century which has seen the upheavals of the great depression and two World Wars, as well as so much technological advance, tastes have had many different environments in which to flourish. While many will instantly associate the name of Carlton Ware with their celebrated lustre wares of between the two wars, or perhaps with their wide range of floral and fruit embossed wares, the actual scope is far wider than these alone.

'Delicacy and simple charm'
Look out for the now rare examples of the earliest work. There are the day-to-day Blush, or Vellum Wares, with their delicate patterns and period charm, many of them purchased for actual usage. In addition, at the top of the market some extraordinarily elegant vases, bowls and tea sets were specially made where the blush was shaded into gleaming dark cobalt blue, and flower patterns, rims and feet were lavishly gilded. At the same time the factory branched out into Sprigged Ware, reminiscent of Wedgwood with pale green classical figures and ornaments applied in relief onto dark green vases and teapots.

You can examine the delicacy and simple charm of W & R Crested, or Heraldic Ware, started soon after 1900, and reflecting both the growth of the seaside holiday and the conflict and changes wrought by the First World War. These items all had their shields and heraldic devices enamelled by hand, and are miniature masterpieces of precision painting.

From the same period look out for the more ponderous, dignified appeal of the matt black wares, lightened by delicately wrought transfer pictures of storks and blossoms. Some of these may feature hexagonal shapes, and silver, or silver plated mounts reflecting the tastes of the Edwardian period, while some show the bold gilt outlining of Wiltshaw and Robinson's cloisonné ware.

'A fantasy world of dragons and birds'
Once past 1920 and the wonders and diversity know no bounds. Lustre wares were produced in a dozen or so colours, and with patterns which initially varied from life-like flowers and butterflies, as in the delicate pre-First World War 'Armand' lustre designs, to an exotic world of Oriental mystique, which pandered to popular fascination with topics like pagodas and temples peopled with oriental figures. This interest in remote places and cultures reached a crescendo with the discovery in 1922 of the tomb of the pharaoh Tutankhamun in Egypt. A new set of designs bearing ancient Egyptian motifs and heiroglyphs appeared in 1923/24 to satisfy this demand. The lustre ranges continued to expand, journeying through a fantasy world of dragons and birds of paradise, and embracing the stunning stylised and abstract designs of the high Art Deco and the Jazz Age.

In the late 1920s, following the surge of more daring expression after the 1925 Paris Exhibition, W & R's craftsmen developed some of the best examples of fantasy designs utilising multi-layering. In patterns such as **Paradise Bird and Tree**, brilliant use was made of underglaze enamels and lithographic transfers. In the finest examples these possess tremendous depth shining up through successive layers which added lustrous glazes and gilt outlines, with highlights in bright top enamels providing the finishing touch.

As the 1920s gave way to the 1930s, Carlton's designers revelled in a series of abstract designs, where the asymmetric blended with the geometric, still utilising recognisable elements from the real world. Fantastically stylised and painted geometric flowerheads cartwheel across space in the fabulous pattern known as *Bell*. A more tranquil mood is expressed in **Flower and Falling Leaf**, while jagged lightning and spiky, jostling leaves grab attention on **Jazz** and *Scimitar*. Echos of the Egyptian discoveries achieve new expression in the elaborately hand enamelled pattern called **Egyptian Fan**, and one of the most striking of the mythical bird designs, again brilliantly combining underglaze and overglaze colouring features fantastically contrived foliage and bird standing beneath with outstretched wings. This rare deco pattern is sometimes popularly called *Road Runner*, or *Secretary Bird*.

As the decade progressed, so designs diversified still further to include on the one extreme, natural subjects, beautifully presented such as **Nightingale** and **River Fish**, and on the other patterns which were purely abstract, with the squares, bands and chevrons of *Mondrian* and **Jazz Stitch**.

From Salad Ware to Handcraft

In the mid-1920s moulded lettuce leaves decorated with bright red lobsters and crabs first made their appearance. With many variations these 'Salad Ware' items were to continue in production right up to 1976, when Public Health regulations banned the red paint used for the lobsters because it contained lead. From 1929 the high glaze wares were augmented by the gentler, more folky look of the matt finished Handcraft pieces, often in softer browns and blues; and the first ever range of 'Oven-to-Table' ware was introduced by Carlton – still effective today if in good enough condition. Pretty, pearlised table china came in, and simple banded wares intended for daily use, as well as the prolific sets of fruit and floral embossed designs; **Oak** and **Buttercup**, **Wild Rose** and **Blackberry** – and many more. During the 1930s many luxury items made their appearance, with boxed coffee sets and figurines vying with wall plaques and cruets, all highly attractive in their own way.

Among Carlton's better known output the range of some twenty or more bone china figurines seem almost out of place – and strongly reminiscent of similar figures from Royal Doulton. In fact they were bought in from Coalport in biscuit form, and glazed and decorated at Copeland Street! In 1937 the factory produced the unique Glacielle range, attracting even royal patronage. This featured mainly animal studies, and had a specially developed, frosted, matt glaze which was said to 'resemble melting snow.'

'Acclaimed Royales and post-war novelties'

After the war lustre wares were still produced – many acclaim the Royale ranges where even a plain lustred and gilded dish is a worthwhile acquisition. Royales may be Vert,

Bleu, Noire, (green, blue and black) and of course the famous deep red Rouge Royale. Decorative patterns included reissued versions of the famous Chinoiserie designs of the 1920s, with their pagodas, temples and islands; and new and attractive designs like *Spider's Web* and *Sultan*, as well as the beautifully enamelled Mallards and Iris flowers to be seen on the pattern known simply as **Duck**. These designs, which moved the Carlton output away from the far-out and stylised designs of the Art Deco period to more naturalistic representation of their subject matter, included many by Rene Pemberton, who joined Wiltshaw and Robinson before the Second World War, and who is still taking an active interest in the enthusiasm for Carlton Ware today.

1950s and 1960s lines like the twin-tone leaves, the **Windswept** range of table ware, and the rarer Pinstripe were accompanied by new embossed ranges such as **Grape** and **Poppy**, **Magnolia** and **Convolvulus**. In 1955 the first of the Guinness advertising wares made their appearance, and soon the range was increased to include the 'Zoo' and variants on the Toucan theme. These were succeeded in turn by the designs of Roger Michell and Danka Napiorkowska starting with the amusing Walking Ware ranges in the 1970s, and many other novelty items reflecting in pottery popular consumer products of the day, such as the Hovis range, Fluck and Law designs (of Spitting Image fame), and pop art ice creams and sundaes.

1990s Carlton Ware
Not quite last in this review of just some of the diverse aspects of Carlton production are the items produced by Grosvenor Ceramics in 1990/92. There are late versions of several of the lustre items ranging from slender bud vases to ginger jars, mainly in dark red. These seem to possess too perfect a glaze, and a more sparse decoration, though the pattern is recognisable.The **Moonlight** range was also produced in a lustrous dark aubergine tint, but with underglaze decoration of Irises. There were also lots of novelty teapots repeated from earlier incarnations.

Francis Joseph – and a new dawn
Finally, just when many thought that the Carlton saga was at an end, the famous marque, found a new and dynamic home. Purchased in 1997 by Francis Joseph, the Carlton Ware name lives on, and two new series of figurines are the first productions proudly bearing the celebrated backstamp. The first of these new series, to be known as the **Carlton Kids** are nursery style figures, some in military dress, made from original 1940s plaster moulds. The second series of Francis Joseph figures are entirely new, and in many cases are planned to echo famous Carlton themes of the past, with **Hollyhocks** and **Mephistopheles** already available. These new pieces are produced to all of Carlton Ware's historical standards of style and quality, but are nonetheless a completely fresh chapter in the story. They too are assured of a valued future with collectors delighted to see that the story goes on.

Building a collection – concepts and costs

Most people find that they have started a collection by accident. They may have been left a few pieces that they like, or received a novel gift and wanted to find out more – or frequently they have acquired a mixed bag of odd items which somehow took their fancy at one time or another, and which cry out to be put into order. However it may come about, whether by accident or design, most collections are fairly random affairs at the start.

Sooner or later, however, you will feel the beginnings of fascination with a pattern, or a particular colour, or a range of designs, and will want to develop a real, more specialised collection. The problem with Carlton Ware is not what to collect, but what to leave out! Since you have got as far as this book you will already have realised that the potential range is so great that it is beyond the means, and the limits of physical space for most people to collect everything. With this in mind, it may be useful to look at a few guide lines before getting in too deep.

First of all, cost . .
One of the joys of collecting Carlton Ware is that it is still possible to build a collection which will give you real pleasure from items costing only a few pounds. Indeed, any collection will flag, or seem like a millstone round your neck if individual pieces represent too much of an outlay. Carlton Ware can be found ranging from a couple of pounds for a simple crested item, up to a few thousand for a *Mephistopheles* bowl. Most items fall comfortably within these extremes.

And where will you put it . .
The second consideration is space (and the bodies within it). Bigger items not only require more space, but are more difficult to display, and more difficult to protect. If your household contains pets and active children then valuable, larger items will need to be confined to certain areas (like higher levels) or specific rooms where the children do not go. Collections have a habit of spreading, so it may make sense to consider what space you can allocate to the collection, and whether you will need to acquire display cabinets, or even to put up special shelves which are out of harm's way. We have encountered collectors who have allowed their prize possessions to occupy part of the treads of their staircase – but few would wish to take such a risk.

Do not be too random . .
Carlton offers a hugely varied choice – but you will find that a group of items of one pattern and colour together looks far more attractive and impressive than a lot of single, disparate items. This applies strongly to some unexpected ranges. Many people collect the well known floral embossed sets, and they display to advantage whether on a sideboard or dresser, or in a cabinet. However try to see a group of early matt black items, with their patterns of peonies or prunus, peach blossom or storks. Singly they are insignificant, but together they are a delight to the eye, relaxing and dignified. Similarly some of the later designs manufactured in the 1950s and 1960s are capable of making a really attractive display when grouped together after a series of visits to local Fairs.

Follow your own tastes, not other peoples.
Above all buy pieces that you like, for in this way you will get together a collection which you will continue to enjoy as it grows, and which has a united feel about it. If you try to follow the ideas of others you may end up confused, and your collecting will be full of uncertainty instead of confidence and fun.

Collect to a theme . . .
How will you set about building an interesting collection? One way is to go for a theme. Carlton made an amazing variety of cruets, for example, and some collectors specialise in these to good effect. Novelty teapots, lustre jugs, chinoiserié plates, toast racks and of course Walking Ware all make excellent and absorbing themed collections at different levels of expenditure. And did you know, for example, that Carlton made a set of mugs with the faces of Coronation Street characters in the 1980s?

or collect by colour . . .
Understandably popular among collectors of lustre items is the idea of grouping things with a common background colour. The Royale finishes, introduced at the beginning of the last war, and developed with great success in the 1950s lend themselves particularly well to this treatment. The deep red Rouge Royale is perhaps the best known as the factory made more of this colourway than any other – but a group of Bleu, Vert or Noire Royale items look spectacular together, and have the added benefit that they will take you longer to assemble, with more visits to Fairs!

Here are a few more ideas for collectable Carlton Ware, arranged to give some idea of the range of prices you can anticipate.

Crested Ware Many items are still to be found costing as little as £5/$8, though rarer and more complex pieces will cost £40-£50/$65-$80 each, with a very small number going over £100/$160. Crested Ware can be acquired, either to a theme such as Animal studies, or Great War memorabilia; or one involving a particular area. If you live in Sussex, for example, you might seek out only items originating in Brighton, Eastbourne, Arundel and other Sussex towns. However it is as well to put in a word of advice. You will see the same item with many different crests on it – and values vary considerably according to the crest displayed. As a broad rule, crests from small towns and villages fetch a higher price than those from the big Victorian resorts such as Yarmouth and Blackpool, where early volumes sold were great. In addition, a piece may be found with a poem or quotation on it, or without – again values will vary. All of these details make collecting Carlton Crested Ware a thoroughly absorbing hobby!

Post-War Ranges Just becoming more sought after, the Carlton output of the late 1950s and 1960s such as **Pinstripe**, **Hazelnut**, **Magnolia** and **Convolvulus**, and even the Table ware sets like the **Windswept** range are collectable today, and likely to become more so as time goes by. Again, a group of matching pieces together will surprise you with how attractive they look. Prices start at about £10/$16, with many pieces valued between £15-£30/$24-$48. They are sure to improve with time.

Walking Ware items start from a few pounds, and vary considerably as collectors are willing to pay £70–£80/$110-$130 for a rare individual piece. Be careful with Walking Ware though, there are at least four differently decorated sets, (including Original, Caribbean, Running Jumping and Standing Still and Big Feet) as well as Circus and countless individual novelty items – you may end up with a lot of little walking feet! Additionally the moulds are still in use by the Price Kensington factory who bought them in 1992. Always check the backstamp to be sure of genuine 1970s Carlton items. The 1970s items normally bear a backstamp which includes the words 'Lustre Pottery' and the actual year of manufacture. Lustre Pottery was the trade name of the company started by Roger Michell and his wife Danka Napiorkowska, the inventors of the Walking Ware designs. These designs, and their originators were taken up by Carlton Ware Ltd. in the early 1970s, and more information can be found in the Chapter titled 'The Story of Carlton Ware'. Walking Ware items are still very reasonably priced, and still retain the humorous touch which made them so appealing when they were first introduced.

Cruets were manufactured from the 1930s right through to the 1990s, and make a fascinating collection. There are fruit and vegetables, birds, dogs and musicians, footballers and golfers. Additionally, cruet sets were produced as part of many of the tableware ranges, such as **Apple Blossom** and **Foxglove** from before the Second World War; **Windswept, Leaf, Hazel Nut** and **Convolvulus** from the late 1950s and 1960s. Prices start at about £15/$24 for a 1960s twintone leaf set, and range through about £80/$130 for a 1930s Crinoline Lady set up to £180/$290 for the Footballer set in mint condition.

Floral and Fruit embossed patterns were numerous, and are deservedly popular for their detailed, life-like mouldings and their pretty, handpainted decoration. First produced in about 1930, patterns include **Rock Garden, Fruit Basket, Apple Blossom, Foxglove, Red and Black Currants, Raspberry** and **Blackberry, Hydrangea, Buttercup** and **Water Lily** as well as others. When you consider that several of these were made in more than one colour, the potential for collectors is vast indeed. Prices vary in accordance with the rarity of the particular range. **Pink Buttercup**, for instance was not made in great volume, and so is rarer, and dearer, than the more common Yellow variety. Prices are 30 to 50 per cent higher for Pink items. Similarly **Foxglove** was made in a wide choice of shapes with both yellow and green backgrounds, and prices range from about £15/$24 for a small dish up to £115/$185 for a cocoa mug with lid, and £150/$240 for a big jug. Now and again you may come across the **Foxglove** pattern with a pink background, and blue foxgloves. Be ready to pay a bit more for this unusual item!

Victorian and Edwardian Ranges These include Blush Ware and the matt black wares which progressively replaced them. As these are some of the oldest of Wiltshaw and Robinson's output it pays to be particularly careful about condition. In their early days many of these items were in daily use, and so chips and cracks were bound to appear. For the sake of making an interesting and varied collection it may be as well not to exclude some small damage (a little rubbing of gilt edges, for example, or a small chip which does not show) but make sure condition is reflected in the price. Small vases and plates will cost from about £30–£60/$48-$96, while a tall temple jar or grand comport may well be worth £150-£250/$240-$400. If you are lucky enough to discover any of the rare blush and cobalt blue glazed bestwares of this period, enjoy the elegance and delicacy of these designs – but be prepared to pay £300-£400/$480-$640 for a nice example!

Chinoiserie This is the name given to the wide range of luxury items with mock Chinese motifs which were first made by the Copeland Street factory in about 1916. Public response was such that the designs proliferated during the 1920s, appearing on a wide range of items, and were revived in the post-war years, even surviving in simplified form at Grosvenor Ceramics in 1990/91. Initially the Chinese designs were featured on handsome matt black pieces with elaborate gilded outlining, and decorated friezes in ivory, terra cotta or emerald green. The designs depict a series of imaginary oriental scenes with pagodas, bridges and temples, as well as 'chinese' figures. The pieces are commonly finished with detailed hand painting on top of the gilt transfer. This was executed to a very high standard in a range of bright colours, and makes the pieces very ornamental indeed.

After a few years the matt black pieces were supplemented by producing the chinoiserie patterns on Carlton's superb lustre and high glaze backgrounds in powder or electric blue, deep red and green, and in the post-war period they can be found on pale yellow and green as well as the 'Royale' lustre finishes. The principle chinoiserie designs were originally the work of Horace Wain who joined the firm as senior designer three years before the First World War, and whose influence was to be considerable over the next fourteen years. A design featuring pagodas, one of which has a post and rail fence, and showing fern-like foliage bore a special backstamp replicating original chinese markings was called **Kang Hsi**, and appeared around 1916. This may be the earliest in the series, but was soon followed by **Mikado**, one of the best known of all the chinoiserie designs, appearing on an enormous variety of pieces in a wide range of sizes and colourways, and characteristically featuring a pair of 'kissing' lovebirds in flight. This was soon joined in the early 1920s by **Temple**, where the chief building shows a view of the interior through a big, circular portal, and **Barge**, where a long, punt-like vessel lies in the foreground, and a few years later by the hugely popular **New Mikado**.

Like the others, this design features a number of different elements, including two distinct pagodas on large islands with overhanging trees, flying storks, and an ornamental bridge arching between tiny islets. These various elements lent themselves to being 'borrowed' for use as separate pictures on many of the smaller items from Wiltshaw and Robinson's repertoire. This habit of utilising small ingredients, or sprigs, from a bigger picture was extended to all the chinoiserie designs to some extent, and has caused many collectors problems with identifying chinoiserie pieces. However, study of the whole designs on larger pieces will reward the patient collector, who will quickly become adept at spotting the smaller element which seems to be a different pattern, but which is, in fact, 'part of New Mikado', or 'part of Temple'.

Chinoiserie pieces from both early and late periods go well together, and may be collected by pattern, such as **Mikado**, or **Temple**, by background colour, or by shape. Plates in chinoiserié patterns make a fine display, and can be stood on shelves or wall hung. They will cost from £40/$65 to £140/$225, while vases range from about £50/$80 up to £350/$560, a good charger may be £300/$480, and a large ginger jar can make £400/$640 plus. In addition there are many smaller items such as ashtrays costing as little as £30/$48.

Handcraft First produced in 1929, and then throughout the 1930s, these matt glazed, hand painted pieces include many different shapes and designs. The Carlton Ware script mark on Handcraft pieces is normally blue, contrasting with the black form on lustrewares, though whether this was deliberate, or the result of a reaction with the type of glaze employed to give the matt finish is open to discussion. Most Handcraft pieces are painted in soft colours, greens and blues, yellows and browns, and depict stylised flowers or completely abstract designs. A few, however, are bolder and much more striking, and these usually command the highest prices.

Now highly collectable, individual Handcraft prices start at around £50/$80 for a small vase, rising to £400-£600/$640-$960 for major pieces. Such a wide range of prices is in part accounted for simply by limited overall supply, as none of the Handcraft production in the 1930s was of great volume. However, some designs, notably those using blue and yellow on a white ground, such as **Shamrock**, *Floribunda*, and **Flowering Papyrus** are fairly common, and therefore reasonably priced. Other, more elaborate designs were produced in very small quantities – sometimes only one or two at a time, as in the case of some of the high fashion Art Deco coffee sets. These more colourful and scarce items are understandably rare and sought after, and prices reflect this.

Fantasy Designs From the late 1920s the boughs of blossom and naturalistic parrots and magpies were progressively replaced by a fascinating series of brightly coloured, fantasy scenes, where exotic birds of paradise flew among strange stylised trees of weird shapes, and with multicoloured foliage. **Chinese Bird, Forest Tree, New Chinese Bird and Cloud, Paradise Bird and Tree** and **Dragon and Cloud** all belong to this phase.

Backgrounds vary from pale beige, through yellows and greens to powder blue and deep lustre red. A particular feature of this group of designs is the superb use of underglaze enamels of very rich colours. These are given depth by the superimposition of gilt outlining, and by the use of overglaze enamels to create highlights. Prices for good pieces reflect their quality and the work which went into creating them, and vary from £250/$400 upwards.

Art Deco and the Jazz Age In the early 1930s Carlton Ware entered its most splendid age. With the exciting Art Deco images from the 1925 Paris Exhibition of Decorative Arts as a driving force, designers in many fields experienced a liberation of ideas, and used previously unheard of boldness in their designs. This explosion of expression occurred nowhere more strongly than in decorative ceramics, with names like Clarice Cliff, Carlton Ware, Shelley and Susie Cooper in the front rank. It would be impractical to describe individual pieces here – many are illustrated elsewhere in this book, and some of the different facets of the range produced are explored in the chapter on 'The Diversity of Carlton Ware'. However during this period were produced a blizzard of abstract and stylised designs, often against Carlton's stunning lustre finishes, and with bright enamelling executed to the very highest standard. *Mandarins Chatting*, **Sketching Bird** and **Spangled Tree, Egyptian Fan** and **Flower and Falling Leaf**, exciting **Jazz** and superlative designs like *Bell, Babylon* and *Secretary Bird* – these evocative names are just a sample of the profusion of Art Deco delights which appeared during the 1930s. A few small items, such as ashtrays or single coffee cans can be found for less than £100/$160 these days – and the largest pieces and rarest patterns may well exceed £1000/$1600. The record to date is believed to be held by a 26cm bowl with the figure of Mephistopheles in red upon a turquoise ground sold in August 1997 for £4700/$7520!

Know what you are looking at

Regardless of what pieces you prefer, whether you collect by period, by pattern or by colour it is important to feel that your money is being well spent. Experience will come with time – but right from the start it is extremely annoying to purchase a piece described as '1930s Carlton Ware' only to discover later that (a) it has been restored, (b) it was made in the 1960s, not the 1930s, and (c) your friend has found a hairline crack on the rim which, in your enthusiasm, you missed. With the right technique you can avoid the embarrassment and annoyance of such revelations.

Do defects matter?
Carlton Ware pieces vary from almost new to over one hundred years of age. Many were originally sold for daily use, not as decorative items, and so naturally some wear and tear has taken place. Does this matter? The important thing is to get such wear and tear into perspective. An otherwise perfect jar, with its pattern intact, but with a little rubbing of the gilt on the rim is still highly desirable, and well worth buying. Point out the rubbing, get a few pounds off the asking price, take it home and be pleased. After all they are not making them any more, are they? And you might wait a long time to find another. On the other hand if major sections of the gilt transfer defining the pattern have disappeared then it may be time to think again. If the paintwork is in good order, and the lustre glaze is undamaged then you may feel that it is worth acquiring for its eye appeal – but be sure that such damage is properly reflected in the price.

As you visit the various Fairs, Auctions and Centres it is quite common to come across pieces in otherwise good condition, but with a hairline crack, often to the rim. Reputable dealers will be quick to draw your attention to this – but there are those who will only notice it when *you* point it out – so you must make sure that you do! Handle the piece, look closely all round, inside and out. Is that bit of darkened crazing at the top just crazing? – or does it show on the outside as well? If so it is not crazing at all, but a crack. At this point you have a decision to make. The piece is otherwise perfect – and of a pattern you would really like to own. This is where knowing your values comes in. Such a piece will still look great in your collection, and it still has a value – particularly if it is one of the sought after designs of the 1930s. As a guide you should expect to buy it for about half of the price of an unmarked example. If you do, you have got something that will enhance your collection, and which will still be wanted by other people if, in time, you want to resell.

Spotting Restoration
Before embarking on a career as a 'restoration spotter' it is as well to have at least an outline knowledge of how the restorer sets about his or her craft. Assuming all the bits are there, then first they must be checked as being clean. This sometimes entails removal of 'Do-It-Yourself' glue, and regluing with adhesives known to be chemically compatible with the paints which come later. After this the restorer will fill the minute remaining cracks with a white filler, and heat the item only to a moderate temperature to harden this. Paint must then be applied, taking the trouble to see that it ends up a perfect match after

reheating. Finally, and if needed to achieve a match, gilding and/or a coat of lacquer may be required. The whole process is a long and painstaking one, and if done properly is very difficult to detect.

So what do you look for? First gilding. Original gilt outlines, whether applied by direct transfer or by dusting prepared oil patterning, were achieved using 22 carat gold dust, which was then heat finished and burnished. To date no one seems to have been able to replicate the shiny gold finish thus achieved. Retouched and restored gilt areas are almost always noticeably dull compared to original gilt work. Look for this around rims, and on projections which get rubbed and broken like feet and handles.

Second restored cracks. If these have merely been glued you can normally spot them, especially in lighter coloured pieces. If professional restoration has been carried out spotting is more difficult. There are pretty fool-proof tests such as X-Ray, though this requires access to specialised equipment which is costly, to put it mildly. There is the 'Paint Stripper Test' which works – but you need to be protected by written permission, or a 'Guarantee of Non-restoration' from the owner or vendor before you put Paint Stripper onto an expensive piece of Carlton Ware to see if some of the enamel will bubble and peel off! If it does not, by the way, then your suspicions were groundless, and the piece is OK.

Eyes, fingers and the 'Ping' test
For most purposes use your eyes and fingers, and employ the 'Ping' test. Sight along edges and round curves to make sure they are smooth and regular. Look for changes in background colour or texture, or small bumps which might be concealing a mend. If you see an area completely free from crazing in an otherwise well crazed article, then get suspicious. Hold the piece carefully and flick the side with a fingernail. It should 'Ping' clearly. If the result is a clonk or a dull thud, then again investigate further – or simply walk away.

Lastly you can obtain an ultraviolet torch. Similar to the lights in discos, and to the devices used for examination of bank notes, these emit UV, or 'black' light which will cause any white filler to show up with a fluorescent glow, even from behind paint. These are not terribly expensive – and could save you from a costly error.

Should you buy it?
Now that you have gone to all this trouble, and you find that a piece you really like has been restored – should you buy it? This decision is completely yours. As time goes by it may become impossible to find a particular piece in original. mint condition. If a piece has been obviously and poorly restored then leave it alone unless you are offered it 'for a song'. However, if the restoration has been professionally done, and is of high quality workmanship – and you are satisfied with it – then there is no reason not to buy. Be prepared to pay a bit less than for a perfect piece – but do not necessarily expect a huge reduction. Professional restoration is a skilled and expensive operation, and can easily cost a three figure sum for a repair of any size.

Re-issues, Reproductions and Counterfeits

Because of the popularity of many Carlton Ware items from time to time there have been re-issues by the factory, and attempts at fraud by people with no authority whatever to produce Carlton Ware. It may be as well to define the various possibilities.

Re-issues

Re-issues by Carlton Ware's owners some years after the original production runs took place on a number of occasions. Some moulds and patterns used to make lustre designs in the 1920s and 1930s (notably some of the popular Chinoiserie patterns like **Mikado** and **New Mikado**, also **Paradise Bird and Tree**) were reused in the 1950s by Wiltshaw and Robinson/Carlton Ware Ltd., and again in the early 1990s by Grosvenor Ceramics, though with reduced pattern. Similarly cruet designs first produced in the 1930s were made again during the Arthur Wood era of the 1970s, and again in 1990/91 by Grosvenor. Some floral embossed patterns, notably Apple Blossom, first made in 1938, were recreated under Arthur Wood in the late 1970s, often with the introduction of some new shapes. Novelty teapots also had two periods in production, in the 1970s and the early 1990s.

None of the above instances are either fakes or reproductions. All of the items produced by re-issue as above are genuine Carlton Ware, as all were made by the official owners of the name, patterns and moulds at the time.

While all of the Carlton items legally produced under the various phases of ownership are both genuine and collectable, it is important to be able to distinguish between them as values will differ considerably. In many instances it will be possible to see the decisive differences once you know what to look for. Post-War lustre wares, for example, are of slightly different colouring. The later blue and green grounds are somewhat darker than those of the 1930s, and are smoother and more uniform – the earlier versions having a slight grain in them, perhaps due to different aerographing techniques, or to coating the pots with powder to generate the colours. Earlier deep reds, too, are often mottled with black, a technique carefully developed with the Aerograph compressed air spraying equipment. The later red typified by Rouge Royale is more uniform in appearance, and shaded to black at the edges.

With novelty wares, such as cruets and teapots, later versions are generally less sharply defined, due to the repeated re-use of moulds, and, particularly in the case of the Grosvenor output, are much less well painted, with less colours being used, and more careless paintwork being apparent.

Read the Backstamp

While the above are subjective differences which you will learn to recognize with experience, there are some concrete points to look for. Always examine the backstamp on any Carlton Ware article. While mistakes were made on the factory floor, the following rules of thumb will help you a great deal:

- Backstamps with the words 'Registered Australian Design' and 'Registered Australian Design Applied For' were used from about 1935 to about 1961 on certain ranges. (See the Chapter on Embossed wares)

- The 'Royale' ranges of lustre wares, Rouge, Vert, Bleu and Noire were only devised in about 1940, and only went into volume production after the Second World War. Any item identified as 'Royale' is not 1930s Carlton!

- The word 'Handpainted' only appeared in backstamps from about 1952 until the early 1960s. Items marked 'Handpainted' are all post-war.

- Up to the early 1970s virtually all Backstamps were applied *under* the glaze. As a result the base is smooth to the touch. Guinness advertising items can be an exception, some having a red mark on top of the glaze.

- Soon after the Arthur Wood buyout they began using a 'Carlton Ware' mark in simple upper and lower case lettering. This was replaced later in the 1970s with a new, small version of the famous scriptmark.

- From the early 1970s onward, and including the output of Grosvenor Ceramics and all known fakes and reproductions, Backstamps were applied as lithographs on top of the glaze, excepting only rubber stamps used by Arthur Wood whose quality (or lack of it) gives them away. You can feel, as well as see, that the stamp is raised above the level of the surrounding glaze.

Reproductions

To qualify as a reproduction an item should :
(a) have been made with the permission of the original manufacturer, or his successors, and
(b) be clearly marked so that the prospective purchaser cannot readily confuse the replica with the original.
To date there is no known bona fide instance of a licensed Carlton Ware reproduction. You may come across items of Guinness advertising ware (Toucans and so on) bearing what looks like a normal Carlton scriptmark with the addition of the word 'Reproduction'. Instances of novelty teapots and the Babycham figure with this mark have also been reported. These are counterfeit items, not genuine Carlton Ware.

Counterfeits

In the past five or six years the rising popularity of Carlton Ware has resulted in some unscrupulous individuals using old moulds of Carlton Ware and then reproducing these items for sale with a fraudulent backstamp. These include a large number of the celebrated Guinness advertising pieces of the 1950s, with the 'Zoo', and both wall mounted and table top Toucans being targetted; some cruets, among them the Crinoline Lady set; a number of the more collectable novelty items, including the JCB Teapot and the Mephistopheles or Red Devil tankard. All of these are counterfeit, or forgeries, being manufactured with intent to deceive, and to obtain money fraudulently.

In general terms all of the counterfeit items suffer from some loss of definition in their moulding, and paintwork is of a poorer standard. In the case of the Red Devil mug the counterfeits show the devil in black trousers – a big mistake as he was originally all dressed in red! However, the intent to deceive is clear from the carefully reproduced W & R Crown backstamp on the base – except for the fact that this mark had been superseded by the time the Devil mug came out – and it should *not* be on top of the glaze! Among the Guinness Ware look out for the following: Flying Toucans without any feet, and with banded yellow and orange breasts instead of the original careful shading; all the Toucans should show graduated shades of orange on beaks and breasts, not yellow and orange bands; beware also of Zoo animals holding pints of Guinness without proper, deep heads on them, and with other details as painted blobs rather than nicely picked out details and sharp mouldings. The Zoo Keeper should have a moulded baby kangaroo poking out of his apron pocket, and an all green uniform; and the adult Kangaroo a bottle of Guinness in its pouch. The Sea Lion should be black, not grey, and the Ostrich should have clearly shaded feathers and a white neck. The sought after Drayman and wagon should have a creamy white base, not green, and again quality of painting will help you decide.The forged Crinoline Lady cruet is also less well moulded, and is glazed in just one colour, touched in with gilt. There is no gilt on an original, but several colours are employed for face, hands, dress and so on to make this a very attractive set.

Unfortunately the normal rules about backstamps do not help with all the Guinness items. Genuine flying Toucans normally do have underglaze stamps, but many pieces, notably the small Zoo figures can have a red scriptmark backstamp applied as a lithograph on top of the glaze.

Early in 1997, after an undercover operation spread over several months, Trading Standards Officers and Police raided a factory in Longton. Bob Snow was arrested, charged and convicted of deceptively producing Carlton Ware and other valued collectable pottery. Among them were Babycham, Martell and Guinness figures and also Crinoline Lady and Tortoise cruets. There is a strong suspicion that this counterfeiting is still going on, so please be careful.

Dating your Carlton Ware

Sadly, it is all too common to come across wrongly dated Carlton Ware, both in Antique Centres, and at Fairs. To be fair to dealers, they probably handle antique goods and collectables from fifty different makers, and spread over a couple of centuries – so it is not reasonable to expect the generalist dealer to have top expertise in everything. It is also true that dealers know very well that an item from the magic 1930s will sell more easily than one from the 1970s! Bearing this in mind you should have a good knowledge of how to date your Carlton Ware – at least within the categories that you collect.

In the Chapters on The History, and The Diversity of Carlton Ware which appear earlier in this book you will glean some general information about what ranges and types of item were produced during the main phases of the factory's life. In the following sections you will find more detailed information about dates and production runs. With Carlton Ware you should always turn the piece over and look at the base. There you may find several different kinds of mark perhaps including the following:

Backstamps
Backstamps were, and are important to manufacturers of china and pottery to establish their brand name, and the authenticity of the article so marked. To the collector they can also provide useful information about the period in which the article was produced. A number of important facts relating to Carlton's Backstamps are set out in the Chapter headed 'Know What you are Looking at', but a simple chronology may be relevant here.

| 1890–1894 | 1894–1927 | 1906–1927 | Variation on left | Used around 1900 as W&R's export markets were established |

| 1925–c1970 | 1925-1957 | 1929-c1939 | 1935–c1961 | 1952–c1962 |

Carlton Ware ENGLAND	ENGLAND LUSTRE · CARLTONWARE	CALEDONIA HERALDIC CHINA	CAMBRIAN CHINA	Carlton Ware ™ HAND PAINTED MADE IN ENGLAND
c1968–1978	Used on the Walking Ware designs	Marks occasionally found on Heraldic china made to be sold in Scotland or Wales		1997

A number of other, special backstamps were also used on specific ranges or designs, and these include marks specific to cloisonné wares, Armand Lustre Wares, Kang Hsi, Kien Lung and Persian designs.

CARLTON WARE
KANG.HSI
1662 – 1722

1622 KANG HE 1722
COCK & PEONY
REG Nº 665093

PERSIAN
W R
&

CARLTON OVENWARE MADE IN ENGLAND

Paintresses' and Gilders' Marks

These take the form of single initials, and sometimes symbols rather than letters of the alphabet, and you will often find two or three of them. The gilder's mark is easy to spot, because gilt is normally used; and there may be a mark identifying the underglaze painter, and another for the person who applied the top enamels. While these are intriguing as you can spot pieces enamelled by the same hand, they are of no real help in dating as no records are known to have survived to show who used what mark, or when.

Order numbers . . .

On most of Carlton's production between the two World Wars, and some of the pieces made earlier than this you will see either one or two numbers written on in black ink under the glaze coat. These take two forms. If a number is preceded by the letter 'O' and a slash, or indeed a letter and number followed by a slash thus:- 'O/6571' or 'F12/5545', then these are believed to be Order or Batch Numbers, applied to facilitate tracking the progress of individual orders through the factory. It is worth remembering that the decorative 'Bestwares' of Carlton were produced in a huge range of patterns and colourways, and were time consuming and expensive to manufacture. As a result small numbers only were made as samples, and almost all of these pieces were made, or at least decorated to order for each retail outlet. Sadly, again no records have survived from which it is possible to interpret these Order Numbers.

. . . and Pattern Numbers

The second type of number, shown as three or four digits thus: '3889', is the all important Pattern Number, and signifies both the pattern design *and the colour of the background*. Thus 3889 is the Pattern Number for the striking and elegant **Sketching Bird** enamelled on a mottled red ground. This pattern can also be seen with a beige ground, Pattern Number 3890; a cream ground shading into dark blue, Pattern Number 3891; and a pale blue ground, Pattern Number 3907 as well as others. As can be seen it is important to note both colourway and design when trying to establish the identity of a piece – and as some combinations of pattern and colour are rarer than others, this has quite a bearing on possible value.

Among the production of the early years these numbers can be seen as three, (or even presumably two digits), before Pattern Numbers reached 1000. However before the First World War the practice of putting the Pattern Number on the base was only erratically applied and some pieces in the early matt black and many in the blushware eras were never marked in this way at all, although numbers for each design did exist.

Similarly factory practice was altered soon after the Second World War, and marking individual pieces with their Pattern Number was discontinued, probably being considered unnecessary as the variety of colours and number of patterns in use in the 1950s was dramatically reduced, and production methods were streamlined. At this time keeping track of small orders was greatly facilitated by the new 'through-flow' electric kilns, where goods were loaded onto small trolleys for firing, rather than disappearing into hundreds of Saggars in a huge bottle kiln.

Dating with Pattern Numbers
So how can we use Pattern Numbers for dating? On their own they are of limited value, but the intelligent collector will learn to use them in conjunction with other factors such as the shape, style and decoration of the piece; and the Shape, or Impressed Mark as described in the following section. What we do know is that Pattern Numbers were allocated in sequence, and, therefore we have a potential range of numbers from 1 to about 4500 covering a period from 1890 to about 1940. Within this period the rate at which new patterns were introduced varied greatly. An approximation would be as follows:

Dates	Pattern Numbers	Dates	Pattern Numbers
1890 to 1916	? up to 2000	1923 to 1936	2701 to 4000
1916 to 1923	2001 to 2700	1936 to 1940	4001 to 4500

As can be seen, for much of this period pattern numbers were introduced at a rate of about a hundred per year, although it should be emphasised that this is only the average. It does, however provide a rough guide which can be used to extrapolate the approximate year when a pattern number was first made.

During the late Victorian and Edwardian periods many patterns that found favour with the public remained in production for several years. People were using many of the blush items and matt black wares in their daily lives, and so liked to build up sets – and needed to buy replacements for breakages. With the introduction just before the Great War of Armand lustre items and the early chinoiserié pieces Carlton moved into wares intended primarily for decoration, and for much of the next twenty-five years the firm made sure of retaining the public's interest by constantly introducing new ideas and new patterns. As a result, throughout much of the inter-war era patterns were only made for relatively short periods, varying from a few months to two or three years. There were exceptions, of course, and some patterns were re-issued due to popular demand – with the Chinoiserie patterns such as **Mikado** and **New Mikado** being the most obvious examples. These had not just one life, but three or four. However differences in detail and in the background colours employed normally make it possible to discern to which period a piece belongs.

The Impressed mark (or Shape mark)
This takes the form of numbers indented into the base of the item, and was made by

setting these numbers into the actual mould. Impressed Marks identify the individual shape, and do not refer in any way to the colour and decoration which may be applied later. As some shapes were made in several sizes, their marks show this by adding a diagonal stroke and an extra single letter or number after the basic Shape Number: thus 1286/2, and 1286/3 referring to a series of finned, diamond shaped dishes; or 456/D and 456/H, which are just two sizes from a popular, ovoid vase shape.

Impressed marks were taken in numerical sequence by the factory, and so if you know when certain shapes were first introduced it is possible to extrapolate to others from the number sequence. However, because many shapes had long working lives, being used again and again with various forms of decoration, *it is only possible from an Impressed Number to deduce a date when it was used first.*

To take an example: You find a nice conserve pot in the Pinstripe design, complete with its saucer. It bears the Impressed mark 2452 (on all parts, by the way, as they were designed to be sold together). How can you date it? As a collector of post-war Carlton you already possess some of the Windswept design, and this is known to have been launched at the Trade Fair in Blackpool in early 1958, and an advertisement appeared in the Trade Press (*Potteries Review* and *Glass Trades Gazette* for example) in 1959 promoting the new range. Your two plates from the Windswept range bear the Impressed Numbers 2404 and 2426. You can now complete the jigsaw for your new Pinstripe piece, as shape 2452 would also have been introduced in 1958, just after the Windswept items, and would then have continued in production for the next few years.

To lessen the detective work here is an approximate chronology of when a good cross section of Carlton Impressed Numbers were introduced:

Shape Number	Date (approx)	
	1925	First 'Crab and Lobster' salad range
	1926/32	Pearlised tablewares 'Clam', 'Orange', 'Peach'
	1932+	Fruit Basket
1000	1934	
1009-1126	1934	Gum Nut
1014-1174	1934	Anemone
1100s	1934/5	Oak
1237-1353	1934/5	Rock Garden
1284	1934/5	Hangman Mug
1367	1935/6	Lettuce (second range of Salad Ware)
1395-1661	1936/8	Buttercup
1416-1461	1936/7	Tulip
1472-	1936/7	Daisy
1477-	1936/7	Blackberry/Raspberry
1540+88	1937/8	Water Lily
1551	1937/8	Wild Rose
1552	1937/8	Crocus
1603	1937/8	Red Currant
1614-1799	1938/40	Apple Blossom 1
1640-	1938/9	Flowers & Basket
1656-	1938/9	Red Currant
1718-1820	1939/40	Water Lily (+1952)

1747-1832	1939/40	Crocus
1751	1939	Pyrethrum
1754	1939	Clover/Shamrock
1764-	1939-	Narcissus
1768	1939	Begonia
1771	1939	Campion
1812-33	1939/40	Wartime figures (?not produced)
1870-	1940/	Foxglove
1907-44	1940/2	Basket
1946-	1942\5	Chestnut
1953-	1942/5	Clematis
1975-	1943/5	Primula
1991-2158	1940/5	Cherry
1995	1944/5	Wallflower
2000-	1945	Delphinium
2008	1945	Apple Blossom Lamp
2010	1947/8	Poppy
2030+47	1947/8	Late Buttercup
2043-	1948/9	New Daisy
2051-	1948/9	Poppy and Daisy
2086-2264	1950/54	Hydrangea
2195-2254	1953/4	Vine
2268-2304	1954/5	Grape
2300s	1955/6	Guinness figures
2316	1955	Hazel Nut
2359-90	1957/8	Leaf salad range
2394-2438	1958	Windswept range
2419-	1958/9	Pinstripe range
2470	1958/9	Langouste (Crayfish)
2480-	1958/9	Convolvulus
2515-2626	1959/61	Magnolia
2533-	1960	Orchid
2637	1965	Guinness Penguin Lamp
2645-53	1965/6	Carlton Village
2694	1967	Arthur Woods takeover
2705-74	1968	Guinness items
2710-49	1968	Tapestry range
2824-61	1968/9	Military figures
2800s	1969	Persian Tea/Coffee
2850s	1969	Skye Tea/Coffee
2991-2900s	1969/70	Canterbury Tea/Coffee
3002-14	1970	Owl, Bird etc Cruets
3021-	1971	Late Buttercup
3143	1972/3	1st Walking Ware Set
3175-3192	1975/6	Apple Blossom 2
3194-3281	1975/6	Walking Ware
3262-	1978-	Dovecote range
3273-3521	1978/86	Hovis Range
3332	1981	Charles & Di Cup
3373-	1981/2	W.Ware Big Feet range
3489-3502	1985+	Robertson Golly set
3500s	1986	Coronation Street characters

Colour section and price guide

On the pages that follow are photographs of a wide selection of Carlton Ware pieces spanning over a hundred years of production. These pictures are arranged in two sections, the first including many of Carlton's bestware designs and the second showing items from the novelty and embossed ranges. In each section items are shown in approximately chronological order, with the earliest wares such as Blushware first, and items produced since the Second World War towards the end. Many of the pieces shown are identified by their Pattern Numbers which were painted on the bases of most of Carlton's bestwares from the Edwardian period right up to the 1940s. Pattern Numbers were issued in numerical sequence, and therefore provide a good indication of when a design was first introduced. As the public were continually looking for new ideas and patterns, many Pattern numbers were only used for a season or two, and were then replaced. However, some patterns proved of such lasting appeal that they were produced in phases over a long period of time – with the best known examples of this being the chinoiserie designs like **Mikado** and **New Mikado**. Accordingly the pattern number must not be taken as a reliable indicator of the actual date of manufacture.

Where possible each piece has been captioned to show:
(a) The Pattern Number (if known)
(b) Either the factory name of the pattern (in bold type), or a name in common usage (shown in italics)
(c) An indication of the size of the example shown
(d) A guide to the value of the piece in good to perfect condition

Sizes: Pieces have been placed in estimated size ranges as follows:

Small	up to 10cm in height	OR	up to 15cm in width
Small/Medium	10 to 15cm in height	OR	15 to 20cm in width
Medium	15 to 20cm in height	OR	20 to 30cm in width
Large	over 20cm in height	OR	over 30cm in width

Guide prices are provided to assist collectors, and have been arrived at in consultation with a number of experienced dealers and collectors. However they should be treated with a degree of flexibility. It is important to note that actual prices will vary according to condition of the piece, and to market trends in an area. It should also be noted that the guide price for a particular pattern in one colourway often does not hold true for the same pattern in another. In the case of Heraldic items prices vary considerably according to the crest displayed, as crests from small, less known villages and towns are more highly prized than the most common ones from the large Victorian resorts.

Blushware biscuit barrel, and two Dressing Table pieces. Medium biscuit barrel (£160-£190/$300-$400), small powder bowl (£40-£50/$75-$90), small lidded pot (£40-£50/$75-$90). Courtesy Beverley

Blushware biscuit barrel with silver plated mount. Medium biscuit barrel (£150-£180/$275-$375). Courtesy Beverley

Bird on a Bough Cloisonné ware. Medium ginger jar (£350-£400/$675-$800). Courtesy Beverley

Pattern 614 Wiltshaw & Robinson experimented with many styles, here imitating the sprigged ware made famous by Josiah Wedgwood. Medium biscuit barrel (£110-£140/$200-$260). Courtesy Christies

English roses on a lovely Blushware barrel, trimmed with gilt and cobalt blue. Medium lidded storage barrel (£180-£210/$350-$400). Courtesy Beverley

*Pattern 595. Late Victorian grandeur in a large lidded jar with **Peony** pattern (£280-£330/$550-$650).*

*Pattern 624, **Imitation Swansea China** produced at the turn of the century. Medium carafe vase (£450-£510/$875-$1000). Courtesy L. Adams*

*Special backstamp used on the **Imitation Swansea China**. Courtesy L. Adams*

Special backstamp used on designs replicating 17th century Chinese styles.

Carlton Cloisonné Ware backstamp from the late Victorian era.

Pattern 722. A further example of **Stork** pattern on matt green. Small/medium footed vase (£150-£180/$275-$350).

Pattern 723 Cloisonné ware from early in the century showing **Stork** pattern. Medium urn vase (£240-£290/$450-$575), medium teapot (£240-£290/$450-$575), medium water jug (£240-£290/$450-$575).

Early version of the W&R Crown Mark used from c1894 until 1925/27.

New technology was often featured in crested wares, sewing machine (£30-£36/$50-$70), gramophone (£50-£60/$90-$110), motor scooter (1920s!) (£60-£70/$110-$130), charabanc (£52-£58/$100-$105).

Heraldic china featured beautifully enamelled coats of arms – and often homely sentiments. Shamrock dish (£4-£6/$7-$10), sundial (£20-£24/$35-$45), lucky white heather (£5-£7/$8-$12), "Good Luck" armchair (£36-£42/$70-$80).

Pattern 1655 lavish gilding highlights the red poppies and flowers in cobalt blue on this medium jardinière made in 1912, (£350-£450/$650-$850). Courtesy Christies

*Pattern 2134 **Flies**, an early lustre item from the Armand range. Medium necked vase (£300-£360/$575-$700). Courtesy L. Adams*

*Pattern 2134. The **Flies** pattern on a pale blue "Armand' lustre ground. Medium vase (£325-£360/$625-$700). Courtesy Beverley*

Pattern 2151 a fine medium sized footed bowl from 1917-18, Basket of Flowers (£350-£380/$675-$350).

The early 'Armand' lustre wares carried a special backstamp. Courtesy Beverley

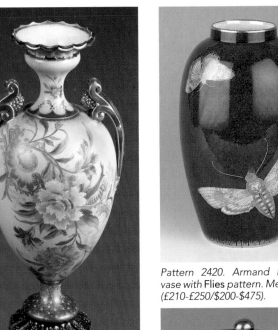

Pattern 2420. Armand Lustreware vase with **Flies** pattern. Medium vase (£210-£250/$200-$475).

Pattern 2250 large baluster jar and cover, with Lion finial, showing the **Cockerels** pattern in enamels and gilt (£275-£325/$525-$625). *Courtesy Christies*

Blushware at its finest in this elegant slender necked vase decorated with carnations. Large blushware vase (£180-£230/$350-$450). *Courtesy Christies*

Pattern 2420 on a small lady's powder bowl with **Flies** pattern (£280-£320/$545-$625).

Pattern 2437, **Fish and Seaweed**, from around 1920. Medium vase (£410-£450/$800-$875). *Courtesy Beverley*

Pattern 2437. Small/medium hexagonal lidded jar showing the **Fish and Seaweed** design (£170-£190/$325-$350).

*Pattern 2519 – the handsome **Barge** design is less common than some chinoiserie patterns Left: large twin-handled footed bowl with blue ground (£300-£360/$575-$700); right large rectangular pedestal bowl (£380-£450/ $750-$875). Courtesy Christies*

*Pattern 2728, a post war example of the popular **New Mikado** pattern. Later blue glaze is darker and less grainy. Medium ginger jar (£240-£290/$450-$575) Courtesy Beverley*

*Left: The series of pieces given the name **Tutankhamen** were produced in very limited numbers to celebrate the discovery by Howard Carter of the pharaoh's tomb in 1922.*
Top: pattern 2706, large shallow bowl with inverted rim (£250-£300/ $475-$575); middle: pattern 2710 large rectangular pedestal bowl with Egyptian motifs in coloured enamels and gilt, (£1300-£1500/ $2500-$3000); bottom: pattern 2710 in gilt only. Large vase (£350-£450/$675-$875). Courtesy Christies

39

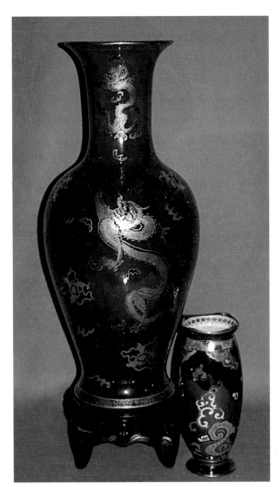

Pattern 2818 **Dragon and Cloud** pattern on a large floor vase with its original stand (£870-£920/$1720-$1800).

Pattern no 2880, a double handed bowl in **Temple**, medium (£115-£140/$200-$250).

Pattern 2922, one of several coffee set designs from the 1920s. Small cup/saucer (£55-£65/$100-$120). Courtesy Beverley

Pattern no. 2884 **Persian** and 2950 **Chinaland**, underglaze designs on electric blue lustre. Large Persian vase (£550-£620/$1000-$1200), small/medium lidded vase (£280-£350/$550-$675).

No pattern number, this vase with its exotic scene has a matt glaze, and may be unique. It is christened Rainforest.

Left: pattern 2932A. Mid 1920s **Stork and Bamboo** with beautiful electric blue glaze. Medium to large footed bowl with pedestal (£500-£560/$975-$1100). Note the word 'sample' on the base of the bowl – perhaps an item provided for a salesman. Courtesy L. Adams

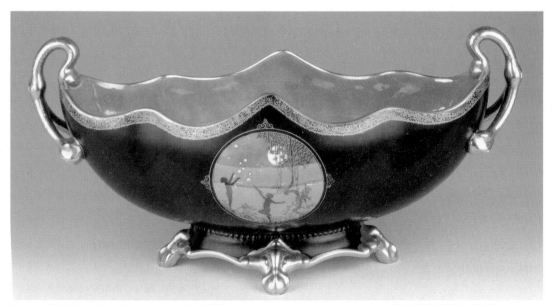

Pattern 2944 Moonlight Cameo on a fine 1920s gondola. Medium/large gondola (£650-£720/$1250-$1400).

*Left: Pattern 2949 **Chinaland** pattern. Very large vase (£750-£850/$1450-$1650). Right: Pattern 3197 **Chinese Bird** on blue, medium vase (£290-£330/$550-$650).*

*A few lustre designs featured elaborate underglaze colouring to create complete landscapes. Left: 2949, large **Chinaland** vase (£750-£850/$1475-$1650); right: 2884 **Persian** vase (£390-£450/$750-$875).*

*Pattern 3026B, **Paradise Bird and Tree** can be seen on many different coloured backgrounds. Medium tray (£290-£325/$550-$625).*

Inverted bowl (£120-£150/$220-$280).

Pattern 3074, a composite design combining swallows and stylised clouds – ingredients of two other patterns. Tree and Swallow and Paradise Bird and Tree with Clouds. Small/medium lidded jar (£390-£430/$750-$830).

Pattern No 3144. **Paradise Bird and Tree** *showing both under and overglaze enamels on this fine gondola. Large gondola (£540-£600-$1025-$1150) and below its backstamp from the late 1920s.*

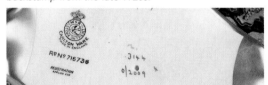

Pattern 3142 **Landscape Tree** *pattern on a coffee cup and saucer. Note orange cup lining. Small cup/saucer (£110-£120/$200-$225). Courtesy L Adams*

Pattern 3145. *Terracotta ground with complex design on this late 1920s pattern. Small cup/saucer (£115-£140/$200-$250). Courtesy L Adams*

Pattern 3154, *one of the most vivid examples of* **Paradise Bird and Tree**. *Medium lidded jar (£550-£650/$1050-$1250).*

Pattern 3158. *A late 1920s variant of the* **Mikado** *pattern. Coffee set (6) (£500-£600/$975-$1200), coffee pot (£150-£180/$275-$350).*

Right and centre: two early examples of W&R lustres from the Armand range, both showing the **Flies** pattern 2112 and 2134. Left: An unusual ginger jar from the late 1920s, **Chinese Bird** pattern 3196 (£750-£850/$1450-$1650), small/medium vase (£220-£250/$425-$475), medium lidded vase (£430-£500/$850-$875).

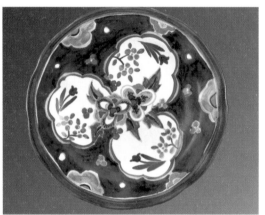

Pattern 3236 a medium sized plate showing the **Floribunda** pattern to advantage (£130-£160/$240-$300). Courtesy Christies

Handcraft preserve pot erroneously marked 3236 (£85-£95/$160-$190). Courtesy Beverley

Pattern 3199. Trinket or stud box featuring Chinese figures and characters. **Chinese Figures** small trinket box (£65-£75/$120-$140).

Pattern 3251 **Dragon and Cloud**, large ginger jar (£480-£520/$950-$1000).

Left: Pattern 3244 **Forest Tree** on a medium bowl (£190-£220/$350-$420); Right: Pattern number indistinct, **Paradise Bird and Tree** large vase (£470-£550/$925-$1050).

Two very similar patterns, 3244 **Forest Tree** and 3285 **Tree and Swallow**. *Medium tapering vase (£300-£350/$575-$675), small squat vase (£275-£320/$525-$625). Courtesy Beverley*

Matt glazed Handcraft items can be bold and colourful like this **Cherry** pattern 3271. Large lidded jar (£750-£850/$1450-$1650).

Pattern 3281, the **Tree and Swallow** design is very similar to Forest Tree. Both occur in various colourways. Small/medium vase (£280-£325/$550-$625).

One of the many colourways for the **Tree and Swallow** pattern 3281. Medium lidded jar (£380-£450/$725-$875).

*Pattern 3279 a delightfully colourful version of **Tree and Swallow** pattern on a coffee set. Complete set for six £900–£1100/$1750-$2150; single cup/saucer £130-£150/$250-$275. Courtesy Christies*

Pattern 3305. A Handcraft pattern sometimes called **Carnival**. Small vase (£220-£260/$425-$550). Courtesy Beverley

The Handcraft backstamp.

Pattern 3354. **Feather Tailed Bird and Flower** design on a blue coffee set. Coffee set (6) (£900-£1200/$1750-$2350), cup/saucer (£120-£150/$220-$275). Courtesy L Adams

Pattern 3334 two pieces displaying the **Geometric Sunflower** design. Large vase (£620-£680/$1200-$1350) and large ginger jar (£720-£780/$1400-$1550).

Pattern number 3353. The famous **Jazz** pattern on orange lustre. Medium lidded jar (£1500-£1800/$2900-$3500). Courtesy L Adams

Pattern 3361, **Jazz** bulbous vase with a blue lustre ground. Medium/large bulbous vase (£720-£800/$1400-$1600). Courtesy L Adams

Left: Pattern 3387, the very decorative Floral Comets design. Cup/saucer (£140-£180/$250-$350).

Pattern 3394 a lady's lidded powder box decorated with the naturalistic **Bird on a Bough** design. Small/medium powder box (£190-£230/$350-$450). Courtesy Christies

Pattern 3388 **Fantasia** shown on a medium to large matt blue vase (£650-£720/$1275-$1400). Courtesy L. Adams

Pattern 3389. Bulbous vase in the **Fantasia** pattern on unusual lilac ground. Medium vase (£450-£495/$850-$975). Courtesy L Adams

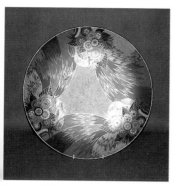

Pattern 3401 Floral Comets, large wall plaque (£850-£1050/$1650-$2050).

Left: pattern 3449 the pattern known as Prickly Pansy on a deep, flaring bowl with three ball feet. **Medium footed bowl** (£300-£400/$550-$750). **Right:** pattern 3655. The factory named this design **Jazz Stitch**. Large ovoid vase (£500-£600/$950-$1150).

Pattern 3406. Three examples of **Fantasia** on dark blue. Small/medium vase (£345-£390/$675-$750), small/ medium biscuit barrel (£345-£390/$675-$750), Bulbous vase (£850-£920/$1650-$1800).

Pattern 3450, Art Deco miniature masterpiece on a ring box, sometimes called Awakening. Small ring box (£280-£320/$550-$600). Inset: Original factory label on base.

Pattern 3451. An unusual vase showing a **Victorian Lady**. Medium vase (£380-£420/$750-$800). Courtesy L Adams

Pattern 3478. **Garden** is the name of this pattern – here on a Rivo shaped bowl (£85-£105/$160-$200).

No pattern number on this unusual charger. It was part of a series, this piece showing a faun among trees (£420-£460/$820-$900).

Pattern 3507. Vivid Iceland Poppy on a matt green background. Medium pot vase (£450-£520/$850-$1000). Courtesy Beverley

Advertising ashtray produced for one of Carlton distributors, small (£80-£100/$000-$000).

An unusual backstamp making clear that Wiltshaw and Robinson were the makers of 'Carlton Ware'.

Pattern 3523. Although Handcraft, this Parkland vase is largely underglaze litho and has gilding to finish it. Medium vase (£470-£530/$900-$10250). Courtesy L. Adams

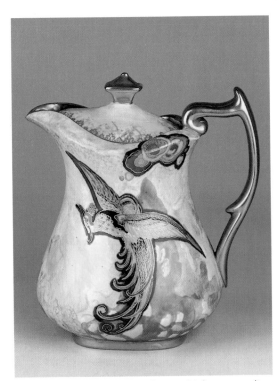

Pattern 3525(?) Chinese Bird pattern on a medium sized ginger jar (£650-£700/$1250-$1350).

Pattern 3525(?). The exotic Chinese Bird on a medium sized coffee pot (£480-£530/$925-$1020). Courtesy L Adams

Pattern 3525 Clematis on a bold Handcraft jug. Medium/large jug vase (£365-£395/$700-$775). Courtesy Beverley

Large pot vase in the Handcraft Orchard pattern (£400 £440/$775-$850). Courtesy Beverley

Pattern 3526, **New Delphinium** shown on a dark blue, matt glaze medium sized bowl (£225-£255/$425-$490).

Pattern 3530. Striking coffee set in Crested Bird and Water Lily. Coffee set (6) (£740-£800/$1450-$1600), cup/saucer (£100-£120/$180-$225).

Pattern 3529, the magnificent Crested Bird and Water Lily on black ground, large ginger jar (£1000-£1200/$1850-$2350).

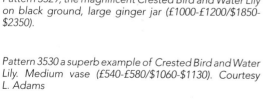

Pattern 3530 a superb example of Crested Bird and Water Lily. Medium vase (£540-£580/$1060-$1130). Courtesy L. Adams

Pattern 3530. Striking underglaze colours feature in the Crested Bird and Water Lily design. Medium bowl (£380-£430/$730-$825).

Outer pair: Pattern 3557 **Fan** on dark blue ground, medium pair of vases (£1000-£1150/$1875-$2250); Inner pair: Pattern 3696, **Egyptian Fan** on dark blue, medium pair of vases (£1200-£1400/$2350-$2750); Centre: Pattern 3695 **Egyptian Fan** on dark red, medium vase (£600-£670/$1175-$1300); Front: Pattern 3695 **Egyptian Fan** on dark red, medium bowl (£380-£420/$730-$810).

Pattern 3695, a magnificent example of **Egyptian Fan** pattern, front and rear view. Medium jug vase (£1200-£1500/$2300-$2950).

Pattern 3547 Diamond, small cup/saucer (£80-£90/$150-$175). Courtesy Beverley

Pattern 3562, coffee cup and saucer in the stunning Nightingale pattern. Small cup/saucer (£175-£200/$325-$375). Courtesy L Adams

Pattern 3552. Unique Art Deco design known as Deco Fan. Coffee (6) (£1500-£1800/$2950-$3590).

Left: Pattern 3562 **Nightingale**, medium bowl (£390-£440/$750-$850); Right: Pattern 4019 **Squirrel** (one of a series), small dish (£190-£220/$350-$420).

Pattern 3562 **Nightingale**. Large vase (£900-£1000/$1750-£1950). Courtesy L. Adams

Pattern 3564. A caddy depicting the rare **Fairy** pattern. Small/medium tea caddy £580-£680/$1125-$1350). Courtesy L. Adams

Right: the Carlton Ware Script mark in use from around 1925 until around 1968, and reintroduced in a smaller variant thereafter.

Pattern 3566 the 'Modern Art' style of decoration merges with Art Deco on this large, twin handled pedestal bowl known as Geometrica (£260-£310/$500-$600). Courtesy Christies

Pattern 3576. The **Fairy** *pattern on a mottled orange lustre ground, medium vase (£870-£1000/$1700-$2000).*

Detail of the **Fairy** *pattern.*

Pattern 3597 shows the colourful **Chinese Dragon** *on a dark blue ground. Medium footed vase £400-£480/$775-$940; Medium slender vase £200-£250/$375-$475.*

No pattern number, and may be a one-off handcraft piece with the title of Over the Rainbow. Large wall plaque (£500-£600/$975-$1200).

Pattern 3601, large trumpet shaped vase (£680-£750/$1340-$1475). Courtesy L. Adams

Pattern 3606, vase showing the Dahlia and Butterfly pattern. Large vase (£810-£900/$1590-$1775). Courtesy L. Adams

Pattern 3651. A magnificent Scimitar footed tray or comport. Large footed tray (£1000-£1200/$1975-$2400). Courtesy L Adams

Pattern 3654. Superb enamelling is the hallmark of the finest Carlton pieces like this double sided vase in Mandarins Chatting pattern. Medium bulbous vase (£750-£900/$1475-$1775).

Pattern 3658. A **Carre** vase. Medium vase (£400-£450/$775-$875). Courtesy L Adams

Pattern 3654. Highly decorated and highly sought after. The **Mandarins Chatting** design on black and green. Small cigarette box (£320-£360/$600-$700).

Pattern 3684, another of the seldom seem Bathing Belle coffee sets, this one on ivory (£1300-£1600/$2550-$3000).

Pattern 3690 Intersection, a rare design from the 1930s. Small cup/saucer (£140-£170/$250-$325), small ashtray (£140-£170/$250-$325), small/medium vase (£520-£600-$1000-$1175).

Pattern 3695. Art Deco vase showing the intricate **Egyptian Fan** design. Small/medium vase (£550-£600/$1075-$1175).

Pattern 3694, **Anemone** shown on two striking pieces, with orange lustre ground. Large charger (£850-£920/$1675-$1800), medium bowl (£450-£520/$875-$1000).

This group shows some of the diversity of handcraft designs. From back pattern 3693 a large wall plaque in **Daisy** *£500-£600/$975-$1175; pattern 3667, rarely seen pattern of exotic lilies, large wall plaque £600-£700/$1195-$1375; pattern 3945* **Tubelined Flowers** *executed in the style of Charlotte Rhead, medium bulbous jug £180-£220/$350-$225; pattern 3458 the Disneyesque Witch's Castle, large vase £250-£300/$475-$575; pattern 3563, bowl with painting of a cottage, somewhat in the style of Clarice Cliff. Medium bowl £500-£600/$1000-$1175. Courtesy Christies*

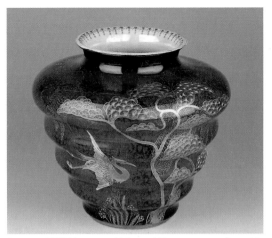

Pattern 3965 Heron and Magical Tree on a medium size interesting tapered vase (£480-£530/$930-$1025).

Left: Pattern 3699, **Rainbow Fan** shown on an orange, footed gondola. Large (£680-£750/$1350-$1475). Right: Pattern 3697, the highly enamelled **Egyptian Fan** on a lilac powder bowl, small (£480-£530/$950-$1025).

Pattern 3765 bright enamelling on a Devils Copse bowl. Medium conical bowl (£690-£740/$1350-$1450). Courtesy L. Adams

Left: Pattern 3719 Mandarin Tree, large vase (£680-£750/$1325-$1475). Right: Pattern No. 4125 **Babylon** medium ginger jar (£600-£680/$1275-$1350).

Pattern 3719, the beautifully hand enamelled Mandarin Tree. Small/medium ovoid vase (£420-£460/$825-$900).

Pattern 3767 Mephistopheles on a lavender ground. Courtesy L Adams

Pattern 3769. The celebrated and rare Mephistopheles figure on a pale yellow ground. Courtesy L Adams

Pattern no. 3786. Deco brilliance with superb enamelling. Two Bell pieces on matt green. The larger jar has been converted into a lamp. Large jar (lamp) (£800-£1000/ $1575-$1975), small potpourri holder (£335-£375/$650-$725).

Pattern 3787, the exotic garden sometimes called Devils' Copse. Large vase (£680-£750/$1325-$1475).

Pattern 3788. The essence of Art Deco. A Bell pattern vase with superb enamelling. Medium vase (£740-£820/$1450-$1625).

Pattern 3787, Devil's Copse shown on two pieces against a dark blue ground. Both large, vase (£680-£750/$1325-$1475), bowl (£390-£450/$750-$875).

Pattern 3788, a striking vase in the sought after Bell pattern on dark red. Medium vase (£740-£820/$1450-$1625).

Pattern 3796. A Bathing Belle coffee set – rare and risque. Coffee set (6) (£1300-£1600/$2550-$3100). Courtesy L Adams

Pattern 3801 spirals of flowers were a popular design feature. Medium conical footed bowl (£390-£440/$750-$850). Courtesy L. Adams

Pattern 3803. Handcraft items sometimes featured bright colours too. Small/medium bowl (£300-£345/$575-$675). Courtesy Beverley

Outer: Pattern 3820, a brilliant pair of large vases in **Hollyhocks** pattern on gleaming black (£1400-£1600/$2700-$3100); Centre: Pattern 3818 **Hollyhocks** again, this time against a green and cream ground on a small to medium biscuit barrel (£450-£480/$875-$950).

Pattern 3813. An unusual goblet in the oddly named **Wagon Wheels** pattern. Small/medium goblet (£800-£900/$1550-$1750). Courtesy L. Adams

Pattern 3820, bowl in **Hollyhocks** pattern on black ground. Medium/large footed bowl (£480-£530/$950-$1000). Courtesy L. Adams

Pattern 3827. Small/medium vase (£280-£320/$540-$620). Courtesy Beverley

Pattern 3815, teacup, saucer and side plate showing the Needlepoint design. Trio (£190-£225/$350-$425). Courtesy L Adams

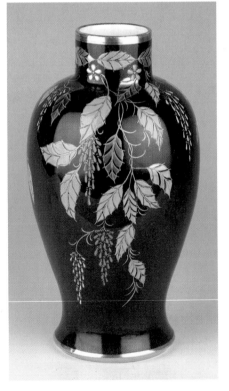

Pattern 3843. Deco shape for this sharp green and gilt dish (£30-£35/$50-$60).

Pattern 3857, a fine vase in **Leaf** pattern. Large vase as shown (£380-£420/$740-$815).

Pattern 3860 **New Mikado** on a dark red ground. Medium/large footed bowl (£130-£160/$240-$300).

Pattern 3863, a miniature masterpiece in the Handcraft pattern **Garden Gate**. Small cigarette holder (£45-£70/$80-$130).

Pattern 3889 **Sketching Bird** pattern on a rare chamber stick (£280-£320/$540-$625).

Pattern 3889. A gem of an ashtray showing **Sketching Bird**. Small ashtray (£95-£115/$175-$215).

Pattern 3889, the oddly named **Sketching Bird** on a rouge jug. Medium jug (£395-£425/$775-$825). Courtesy Beverley

Pattern 3891, the popular **Sketching Bird** pattern on a cream base. Medium pedestal vase (£400-£450/$775-$875).Courtesy L. Adams

Pattern 3891. The factory named this pattern **Sketching Bird** medium vase (£400-£450/$775-$875).

Pattern 3894, delicate and scarce **Persian Garden**. Small preserve pot complete with lid and saucer (£265-£300/$510-$590).

Patterns 3897 and 3896. Decorative posy bowl (£140-£170/$250-$325), small cardholder (£65-£80/$120-$150).

Pattern 3913. A coffee cup and saucer in the Moderne shape with Floral Mist pattern. Small cup/saucer (£45-£55/$80-$100). Courtesy Beverley

Pattern 3923 **Wild Duck**, a mid 1930s design, some five years earlier than the popular **Duck**. Medium bulbous onion vase (£280-£320/$550-$620).

Pattern 3926. Superb detail in the enamelling on two Summer Flowers pieces, medium posy bowl (£250-£290/$475-$550), small squat jug (£320-£380/$610-$750).

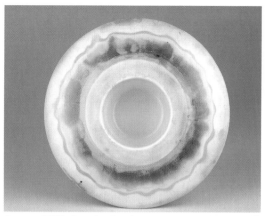

Pattern 3939. Simple slip decoration to a 1930s small/medium posy bowl (£45-£50/$80-$95).

Pattern 3944. Gum Tree in blue/green. Part of the Handcraft range. Small/medium £85-£95/£150-$175).

Pattern 3948, a large charger in **Flower and Falling Leaf** design on turquoise, with a matt glaze (£550-£650/$1050-$1275).

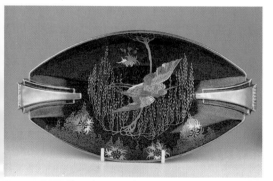

Pattern 3952 **Sketching Bird** pattern on a powder blue Aztec shaped dish (£150-£170/$275-$320).

Pattern 3965, one of the fantasy designs Heron and Magical Tree. Medium/large tray (£360-£400/$700-$780) Courtesy Beverley

Pattern 3965. Art Deco style platter showing Heron and Magical Tree (£360-£420/$700-$825).

Pattern 3965. Heron and Magical Tree on a Rouge Royale vase, medium (£425-£475/$825-$925).

*Pattern number 3949. Two views of the detailed hand enamelling on a vase showing the **Flower and Falling Leaf** pattern. Medium/large vase (£1200-£1400/$2300-$2750). Courtesy L Adams*

Pattern 3967 bulbous vase showing Lace Cap Hydrangea design. Medium vase (£480-£530/$950-$1025). Courtesy L. Adams

Pattern 3972, this witty Art Deco vase with **Hollyhocks** was made to seem as if it was the wrong way up! Small/medium vase (£250-£300/$475-$575).

Pattern 4018. The height of 1930s decoration, Secretary Bird. Small/medium pot vase (£460-£500/$900-$975). Courtesy L Adams

Pattern 4076. Striking Tyrolean Bands pattern on a small to medium sized teacup and saucer (£150-£170/$275-$320). Courtesy Beverley

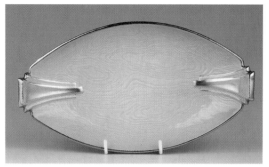

Even a plain green dish with gilt detail has style. Medium dish (£28-£35/$50-$65).

Above: pattern 4017. Two vases showing one of the ultimate deco designs of the 1930s on the rare orange ground Secretary Bird. Small/medium ovoid vase (£650-£750/$1275-$1475), small/medium waisted vase (£650-£750/$1275-$1475). Below on a medium vase (£650-£750/$1275-$1475).

Pattern 4103 **Spider's Web** on a pale green ground. Small/medium bowl and cover (£230-£260/$450-$500). Courtesy Beverley

Pattern 4120, sometimes known as Primula and Leaf, this design often also includes Bluebells! Medium dish (£80-£90/$150-$170).

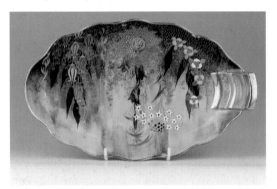

Pattern 4125. The rare and fabulous Babylon pattern, with festoons of tropical foliage. Medium dish (£380-£430/$730-$850).

Pattern 4138. **Tubelined Tree and Fields** imitates the technique of Charlotte Rhead. Medium Bowl (£365-£410/$700-$800). Courtesy Beverley

Pattern 4159, Heron and Magical Tree. Red ground hardly shows behind green tree foliage. Small cup/saucer (£120-£150/$225-$275). Courtesy L Adams

Pattern 4160, two examples of a most decorative variant of Heron and Magical Tree. Very large Temple jar (£1300-£1500/$2500-$3000) and medium dish (£330-£370/$650-$700).

Pattern 4194 (?) Iceland Poppy was used on both tea and coffee sets. Medium teapot (£480-£530/$950-$1025). Courtesy L Ward

Pattern 4215 one of the 1930s geometric designs known as Starflower. Large vase (£690-£780/$1350-$1550).

Pattern 4219 **New Anemone**, *large vase (£540-£600/ $1025-$1175). Courtesy L. Adams*

Pattern 4219, **New Anemone** *dish in the Aztec shape, medium dish (£70-£90/$125-$160).*

Pattern 4225. Coffee cup and saucer in the Rita shape – polka dots on a rouge ground. Small cup/saucer (£60-£65/$110-$120.). Courtesy Beverley

More polka dots on a cream ground on this small cup/saucer (£60-£65/$110-$120). Courtesy Beverley

*Pattern 4244. A smart **Spiders Web** coffee set on deep blue. Coffee set (6) (£550-£600/$1075-$1175), Cup/Saucer (£60-£70/$110-$130).*

Pattern 4242, a fine large **Spider's Web** vase (£510-£560/ $1000-$1100). Courtesy Beverley

Left: Pattern 4244, a small to medium tobacco jar in dark blue showing the popular **Spider's Web** (£260-£290/$500-$575); Right: Pattern 4243, a grand Temple jar in the same design on grey/blue (£490-£530/$960-$1050).

Pattern no. 4244 **Spiders Web**, medium vase (£350-£400/$675-$775). Courtesy Beverley

Left: Pattern 4247 **Rabbits at Dusk**, large vase (£575-£650); Centre: Pattern 2946 Moonlight Cameo small to medium lidded jar (£280-£320/$550-$625), and right: Pattern No 2944, Moonlight Cameo large vase (£300-£350/$575-$675).

A trio of jugs all in the Moderne shape. 4247 **Rabbits at Dusk** *medium jug (£380-£420/$745-$825), 4163* **Spangled Tree** *medium jug (£250-£280/$475-$550), 3975 Persian Rose medium jug (£350-£390/$690-$760).*

Pattern 4247. Glowing lustre in the **Rabbits at Dusk** *pattern. Large wall plaque (£350-£400/$675-$775).*

Pattern 4247. Great depth is created by the lustre glaze on this **Rabbits at Dusk** *vase. Medium vase (£480-£540/$950-$1050).*

Pattern 4283, **New Stork** *pattern in a very unusual variant, with a pink ground. Large wall plaque (£570-£630/$1125-$1240).*

Left: Pattern 3966 **Lace Cap Hydrangea** medium footed bowl (£450-£520/$775-$1010). Right: Pattern 4313, Heron and Magical Tree, medium vase (£360-£390/$700-$775).

Another **New Stork** piece. This pattern was very popular in the 1950s. Medium bowl (£140-£160/$250-$300).

Left: pattern 4340. The **New Stork** pattern also on Rouge Royale. Medium bowl (£95-£115/$175-$205).

Patterns 4328 and 4433. Ever popular chinoiserié items. Large dish, **New Mikado** on cream (£120-£150/$225-$275), footed dish in **Mikado** on Rouge Royale (£75-£85/$130-$150), small ashtray (£55-£70/$100-$125).

Plain Rouge Royale items are attractive and collectable. Medium oval bowl (£45-£50/$80-$90); small/medium vase (£45-£50/$80-$90); small lobed dish (£30-£40/$50-$75).

*Pattern 4433. Two small, later examples of **Mikado** pattern on Rouge Royale. Small pot vase (£55-£65/$100-$120); small ashtray (£50-£60/$90-$110).*

Spiders Web *shown to advantage on a full bodied medium size vase (£380-£420/$700-$825). Courtesy Beverley*

Pattern 4488 a post-war coffee set on Noire Royale showing Lily of the Valley. Coffee set for six £800-£900/ $1550-$1775; single cup/saucer £90-£110/$165-$200. Courtesy Christies

Pattern 4499, Duck *on Rouge Royale. Medium dish (£160-£185/$300-$350).*

Duck *on Rouge Royale. Medium vase (£350-£400/$675-$775). Courtesy Beverley*

Pattern 4499. 1940s Duck *design with bright enamelling and vivid colours. Medium jug (£230-£270/$450-$525).*

Duck *in miniature on a coffee cup and saucer, small (£55-£65/$100-$120).*

Pattern 4499. *The popular* Duck *pattern. Very large Temple jar (£750-£820/$1475-$1625).*

Pattern 4499, Duck *shown to advantage on this large handsome charger (£380-£430/$750-$850).*

A post-war handled vase in Bleu Royale showing simple, mainly gilt design. Small vase (£50-£65/$90-$120), and inset the backstamp. Note also the word 'Handpainted'. In use from about 1952-1962.

New Mikado *(late version) on a Rouge Royale medium bowl (£120-£140/$225-$250).*

Small cup/saucer in **Spider's Web** *(£75-£85/$130-$150). Courtesy L Adams*

Coffee cup/saucer in cream with **New Stork** *pattern. Small cup/saucer (£75-£85/$130-$160. Courtesy L Adams*

Pale blue lustre showing **New Mikado**. *Small cup/saucer (£65-£75/$120-$130). Courtesy L Adams*

Cup and saucer in Bleu Royale colourway (£60-£65/$110-$120). Courtesy Beverley

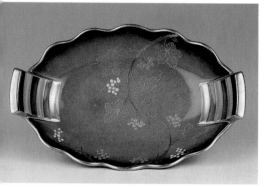

Vert Royale favours the **Vine and Grape** *pattern. Small footed dish (£45-£55/$80-$100).*

Kingfisher on a medium Rouge dish (£80-£100/$150-$190).

Some designs of the 1950s beautifully combine under and overglaze colours, like this **Bullrushes** ginger jar. Small/medium jar (without lid £140-£190/$250-$360; with lid £295-£325/$575-$625).

Sultan and Slave shown on Rouge Royale. Medium bowl (£250-£280/$475-$550), medium vase (£340-£390/$625-$750).

Spiders Web shown on two similar Rouge Royale dishes of different sizes, small (£80-£100/$150-$190), small/medium (£120-£160/$225-$300).

Bullrushes pattern on Rouge Royale, medium vase (£230-£260/$450-$500).

The late Kingfisher design on two Rouge pieces. Medium plate (£100-£120/$190-$225), small/medium ginger jar (£250-£280/$475-$550).

Attractive effect from later Rouge Royale items. Small leaf (£18-£20/$30-$40), medium leaf (£22-£28/$40-$55), medium/long leaf (£18-£20/$30-$40), small cruet (£65-£75/$120-$140).

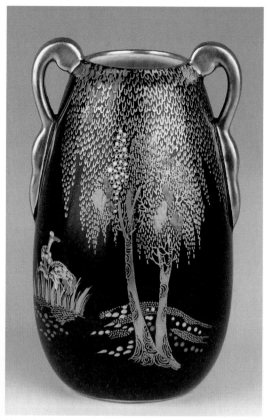

The Rouge Royale stamp on a 1950s trinket box.

New Stork *pattern, popular in the 1950s, on a black background. Small vase £150-£180/$275-$350).*

No pattern number (post-war design), two pieces of **Sultan and Slave** *pattern on black. Medium size vase (£450-£550/$875-$1075) and medium dish (£250-£290/$475-$575).*

Two examples of the very popular **New Mikado** *pattern on the Rouge Royale background, left: large oval pedestal dish showing part of the pattern £180-£230/$350-$450; right: large wall plaque showing the whole pattern £225-£275/$425-$525. Courtesy Christies*

Spider's Web *on a 1950s trinket box, small (£70-£90/$130-$170).*

A deep Vert Royale bowl with Spider's Web *pattern (£180-£220/$350-$420).*

A much later Rouge Royale piece Rosebud. Medium slender vase (£30-£40/$50-$75).

Bleu Royale items from the 1950s, from left, small ashtray/coasters (£30-£40/$50-$75) each; medium bowl (£80-£90/$150-$175).

More late Rouge items from the 1970s. Small/medium spiral vase (£40-£50/$75-$95), small candlestick (£30-£35/$50-$60), small footed dish (£30-£35/$50-$60).

Flowers and Basket preserve pot (£95-£115/$175-$210). Courtesy Beverley

Spiders Web *on a small pink ribbed vase (£90-£100/$160-$190). Courtesy Beverley*

Medium sized footed bowl in **Fruit Basket** *(£40-£60/$70-$110). Courtesy Beverley*

Fruit Basket *Biscuit barrel (£120-£145/$220-$275); Sugar shaker (£90-£115/$170-$200). Courtesy Beverley*

The **Anemone** *range of 1934 was vivid, with a high glaze and strong colours. Medium/large (£75-£95/$130-$175), preserve pot (£85-£90/$150-$175).*

Has anybody got one of these? This drawing from the shape book depicts shape number 1083 from about 1934 and shows a stylish hand mirror.

Rock Garden was matt glazed, in beige or pale blue, moulded with brickwork and a scattering of cottage flowers. Large jug (£120-£150/$220-$275), small vase (£40-£60/$70-$110), jug vase (£70-£80/$130-$150), sauce boat (£65-£75/$120-$140).

By contrast with the matt finish of Oak, the Fruit Basket range had a high glaze finish. Cream jug (£50-£60/$95-$110), toast rack (£45-£50/$80-$90), milk jug (£85-£95/$150-$175).

*Early embossed wares included the **Oak** pattern, with strong bold shapes and made in two colourways, beige for day and blue grey for night. Tripartite dish (£60-£70/$110-$130), charger (£150-£170/$280-$325), nut dish (£15-£20/$25-$35), small toast rack (£40-£50/$75-$95), vase (£60-£70/$110-$130). Also available is an unusual candlestick (£80-£90/$150-$175).*

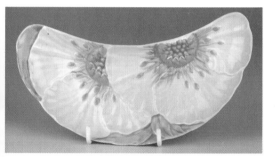

*Yellow **Buttercup** side dish (£45-£50/$80-$95).*

Wild Rose toastrack (£75-£90/$140-$170). Courtesy Beverley

*Embossed jam/butter dishes come in many different patterns, from left: **Raspberry** (£30-£40/$50-$75); **Blackberry** (£25-£35/$40-$60); Yellow **Buttercup** (£25-£35/$40-$60); Pink **Buttercup** (£35-£45/$60-$85).*

From Top left: Unusual box and cover in the form of a lady in 18th century dress £180-£220/$350-$425; 'Joan', one of the figures modelled by Coalport, painted by Carlton £200-£260/$375-$500; Clown with moving head modelled by John Hassall £220-£260/$425-$500; Series of novelty napkin rings: Clown £55-£75/$100-$140; Guardsman £55-£75/$100-$140; Farmer's Wife £55-£75/$100-$140; Sailor £55-£75/$100-$140; Pierrot £55-£75/$100-$140; Crinoline lady £55-£75/$100-$140; Performing Dog £55-£75/$$100-$140. Courtesy Christies

Groups of embossed wares always look well as with the **Blackberry** items: teapot £275-£300/$525-$675; biscuit barrel £145-£175/$275-$340; sucrier £45-£55/$85-$100; cup/saucer £40-£45/$75-$80; cream jug £65-£85/$120-$150. Courtesy Christies

Primula small preserve pot (£60-£80/$110-$150). Courtesy Beverley

These hard to find figurines were cast at Coalport China and decorated by Carlton! (£200-£300/$375-$575 each). Courtesy Beverley

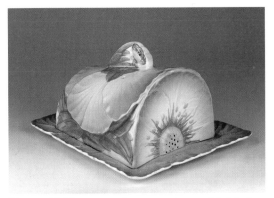

*The rare **Pink** Buttercup shown on a cheese dish. Medium cheese dish/cover (£300-£350/$575-$675). Courtesy Beverley*

Pink Waterlily. *Small/medium grapefruit dish (£80-£95/$150-$175). Courtesy Beverley*

Above: **Raspberry.** *Cream Jug (£70-£85/$130-$160), Bowl (£60-£75/$110-$140).*
Courtesy Beverley

Pink Buttercup, *from left medium tripartite dish (£150-£200/$275-$375); small/medium cream jug (£140-£190/$250-$370); small sugar shaker (£200-£250/$375-$475); small cruet (£150-£200/$275-$375). Courtesy Beverley*

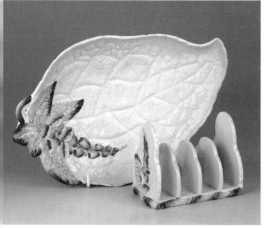

Foxglove *was produced in three colours. Here in pale green, medium dish (£30-£35/$50-$60), toast rack (£70-£80/$130-$150). Courtesy Beverley*

Tripartite dish with **Waterlily** *(£70-£85/$130-$155). Courtesy Beverley*

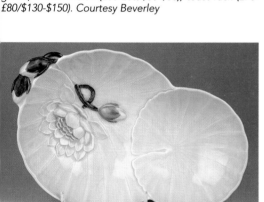

Waterlily *on a two lobed dish (£40-£50/$70-$90) Courtesy Beverley*

An earlier Salad Ware dish from the Lettuce range. Medium long dish (£18-£25/$30-$40). Courtesy Beverley.

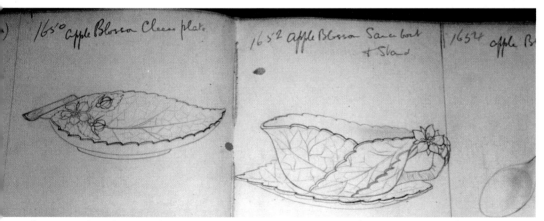

Part of two pages from the original Carlton Ware Shape Book, showing items from the popular Apple Blossom range.

Wild Rose *items in green and in cream. Side plate (£25-£30/$40-$50), plate (£28-£32/$50-$60), preserve pot (£45-£60/$080-$110), cream jug (£40-£45/$75-$80), cup/saucer (£40-£45/$75-$80), jam dish (£15-£18/$25-$30). Courtesy Beverley*

Apple Blossom, *lidded cocoa mug (£110-£125/$205-$240), cream jug (£40-£45/$70-$85), cruet ovoid egg cups (£115-£130/$200-$250), preserve pot (£45-£60/$80-$110). Courtesy Beverley*

Begonia *jam dish (£30-£45/$50-$80).*

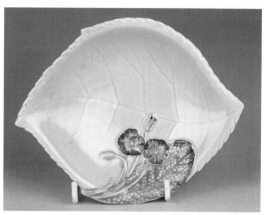

Primula, *small jam dish (£18-£24/$35-$45). Courtesy Beverley*

Campion *butter dish (£25-£30/$40-$55).*

Undecorated **Buttercup.** *Some wartime production was undecorated, and this economy ware was also exported as it avoided certain duty fees. Small jam dish (£20-£25/$35-$40).*

Waterlily, *medium salad strainer (£95-£115/$180-$200); medium teapot (£240-£280/$450-$550); medium fruit basket £150-£170/$275-$325). Courtesy Beverley*

Apple Blossom, *triangular dish (large) (£35-£38/$65-$70), cocoa mug (£85-£95/$160-$180), small cruet (£70-£85/$130-$160), preserve pot (£45-£60/$80-$110). Courtesy Beverley*

Foxglove *items in pale yellow. Sandwich plate (£30 £35/$50-$60), side plate (£22-£28/$40-$55), gravy boa (£45-£55/$80-$100), sugar bowl (£25-£30/$45-$55), coco mug (£85-£95/$160-$180). Courtesy Beverley*

Waterlily *as a Tea for Two set (£360-£410/$700-$800). Courtesy Beverley*

Blackberry. *Teapot (£275-£300/$525-$575); Cream Jug (£65-£85/$125-$150), Sucrier (£45-£55/$85-$100). Courtesy Beverley*

Bowl and salad server from the Lettuce salad range. Medium bowl/server (£60-£70/$110-$130). Courtesy Beverley

Embossed wares were popular over four decades. Here a 1970s addition to the **Buttercup** *range (£90-£95/$175-$190) is shown with 1930s* **Water Lily** *(£240-£280/$450-$550).*

1930s novelty napkin rings **Guardsman** (£55-£75/$105-$140), cat (£60-£80/$110-$150). Courtesy Beverley

Novelty Crinoline Lady napkin rings, small (£60-£80/$110-$150).

A Saladware cruet, small size (£50-£70/$95-$130). Courtesy Beverley

This original Hangman Mug first produced in the 1930s. Fakes have the wrong backstamp and the devil in black trousers. Red devil/hangman mug £125-£160/$225-$300. Courtesy Christies

Introduced about 1959, **Magnolia** was produced in several colourways, and featured contrasting lids. Oval dish (£18/£25/$35-$45), teapot (£35-£45/$65-$90), small dish (£10-£14/£15-$25), coffee pot (£35-£45/$60-$80).

Fruit dish introduced around 1959 showing three sections as apples and pears. Medium tripartite dish (£70-£80/$130-$150).

Pinstripe ranges appeared in 1959 in pale green, rust and beige. Medium tripartite dish (£20-£30/$35-$55).

Hazelnut appeared in the mid 1950s and became very popular. Front dish is in **Convolvulus**. Medium dish (£15-£18/$25-$30), teapot (£35-£45/$65-$85), small/medium dish (£15-£18/$25-$30).

One of the last of the **Langouste** salad items. Note the bronze colour of the lobster as now pigments had replaced earlier lead based red paints. Medium oval dish (£18-£24/$35-$45). Courtesy Beverley

Late 1950s **Pinstripe** in rust colouring makes an attractive group. Two part dish (£20-£25/$35-$45), nut bowl (£12-£15/$20-$25), preserve pot (£33-£40/$60-$75), sandwich plate/cup (£28-£32/$50-$60), butter dish (£35-£40/$65-$75), jam dish (£8-£12/$15-$20). Pinstripe pieces are not numerous, and should gain in value with time.

A wide range of Fruit wares were produced in the early 1960s. Toast rack (£70-£90/$135-$175); jam dish and spoon (£18-£25/$30-$45); coffee pot (£60-£80/$110-$150). Courtesy Beverley

Apple tea service from the **Fruit** range. Teapot (£50-£60/ $90-$110), preserve pot (£25-£30/$45-$55); cream jug (£25-£30/$45-$55), cup/saucer (£28-£35/$50-$65). Courtesy Beverley

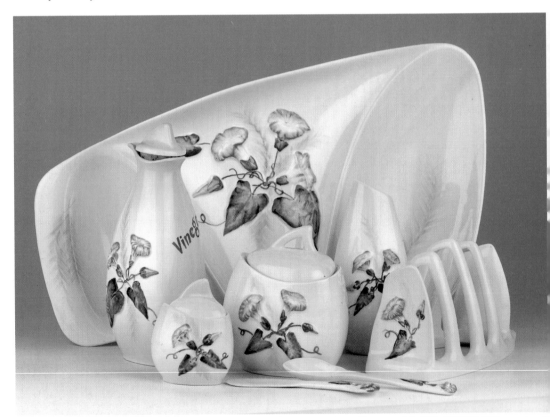

Convolvulus pattern from the late 1950s in the less known lime green. Hors d'œuvre dish (£30-£35/$55-$65), toast rack (£25-£30/$45-$55), vinegar (£30-£35/$55-$65), preserve/spoon (£20-£25/$35-$45), sugar (£22-£28/$40-$50), mustard jar (£20-£25/$35-$45). *Convolvulus* and *magnolia* items are still very reasonably priced – and are sure to appreciate with time.

1950s Guinness Novelty figures, small Toucan with pint glass (£110-£140/$210-$260), Kangaroo (£120-£150/$230-$290), Zoo Keeper (£100-£125/$190-$245), small Sea Lion with pint (£120-£140/$230-$260), Ostrich (£110-£140/$220-$260), Tortoise (£120-£140/$230-$260). Courtesy Beverley

Guinness advertising wares have acquired cult status among collectors – but it is important to avoid counterfeit items. From back left: Toucan table lamp £350-£450/$690-$875; Penguin table lamp £700-£900/$1350-$1750; Large Toucan with pint £550-£700/$1075-$1490; Sealion with globe £450-£550/$870-$1100 Zookeeper £100-£125/$185-$230; Tortoise £100-£125/$185-$230; Ostrich £110-£140/$200-$260. Courtesy Christies

Hydrangea, seen here in two different colourways, is popular with collectors. Oval dish (£60-£70/$110-$130), round platter (£90-£100/$160-$190).

An oyster dish from the **Langouste** range. This third series of Salad Wares was produced in the late 1950s. Large oyster dish (£70-£90/$130-$170). Courtesy Beverley

Two Walking Ware pieces, hot water jug (£80-£100/$150-$195), teapot (£80-£100/$150-$195). Courtesy Beverley

Walking Ware was a huge success throughout the 1970s and is still made today by the Price Kensington factory. Teapot (£80-£100/$150-$195), cups (£25-£28/$45-$55), egg cup (£12-£16/$20-£30), sugar (£30-£35/$50-$60), milk (£25-£30/$45-$55).

A medium sized Walking Ware teapot from the 1970s (£150-£180/$275-$350). Courtesy Beverley

A pair of Walking Ware medium plates (£60-£70/$110-$135 each). Courtesy Beverley

Walking Ware egg cup with cosy (£55-£60/$100-$110) with Red Baron teapot (£150-£200/$280-$375).

1970s toastracks, including one from the Hovis range. (£15-£18/$25-$35 each). Courtesy Beverley

Conserve pot from the 1960s Village range (£75-£85/$140-$160). Courtesy Beverley

100

My Garden – the inspiration for the Hollyhocks figure below (£300-£400).

Collect-It Airman teapot limited edition 100. The first in a series of 10 unusual colourways produced especially for UK shows and exhibitions (£80-£100).

Classic Airman teapot – **Blue Camouflage**. Edition 150

Carlton Girl Hollyhocks limited edition 1250 (RRP £165).

Jester. Second in the Character Series limited edition 500 (RRP £165).

The old. . . .original Carlton Kids from left: Groom and Bride; Airman; Sailor; Nurse (RRP £35 each).

The new . . . Spicegirl, Schoolboy, Policeman and Footballer (RRP £35)

Pidgeon Fancier character jug (RRP £59.99)

Santa Carlton Kid. First in a series of ten to be released each year with a change of toys in the sack. Limited to 200 in the first year.

Negro Band prototypes from 1940 moulds

Red Devil, issued to all inaugural members of the Francis Joseph Carltonware Collectors Club. This cannot be purchased by any other means. To join, see advert at back of this book.

Mephistopheles. First in the Character Series limited to 500 (RRP £165). Inset: Colourway of Mephistopheles. Only a few were produced within the edition of 500

Carlton Girl with Bird of Paradise. Prototype.

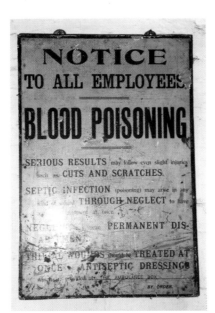

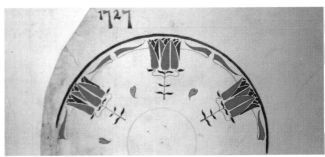

Another pattern, probably Birks, Rawlins & Co. This one shows transitional style between. Art Nouveau and Art Deco.

Lead, mercury and other chemicals made pottery manufacture hazardous to health earlier this century. Courtesy Coalport China Museum

Sadly the Carlton Pattern books have been lost – this illustration shows the great detail in which patterns were recorded. It is probably of a Birks, Rawlins china set. B, R & Co were bought out by Carlton in 1928.

These plates show the range of colours used at Gladstone China. Each factory guarded the secret formula for each of its colour shades jealously. Courtesy Gladstone Working Pottery Museum.

The problems of success – Guinnessware toucan with forged Carltonware backstamp (below). Note inferior decoration.

The making of a vase

To achieve the soft, mellow tones of Handcraft, or the jewel-like brilliance of Carlton's decorated lustre pieces took a long and complex series of operations involving many varied skills. In this chapter we will trace the processes by which one imaginary Carlton Ware vase was produced in the 1930s from raw clay to finished article.

The home of Carlton was, of course, Stoke-on-Trent, one of the famous 'six towns' which were, and still are the heart of the British pottery and china industry. The six towns, Tunstall, Burslem, Hanley, Stoke, Fenton and Longton nestle together in north Staffordshire. It is interesting to reflect, however, that their success was based not on local clays, but on the proximity of large deposits of coal, a necessity for firing the kilns; and of the inland water way system, important both for its water supply and as a means of transportation.

Raw Materials were far from local

The raw material required to make our vase comes from far away in the south-west peninsula. When pottery manufacture developed in the 18th century it initially utilised local clays, but these are quite coarse, and fire to a red colour which is difficult to decorate. By the mid 19th century these red clays did not find favour compared to the white wares which were being imported from China and the Far East. To rectify this the potteries brought in China Clay and China Stone from south Cornwall, and a better, finer clay known as 'Ball Clay' which is only found in north and south Devon, and Dorset.

By far the greatest proportion of Carlton's output has always been Earthenware, although we will look separately at Crested or Commemorative ware in another chapter. Earthenware is typically made from a clay mixture, or 'body' consisting of a combination of ingredients, and our vase needs a mix, or 'body' containing approximately:

25 percent Ball Clay   15 percent China Stone
25 percent China Clay   35 percent Flint.

Ball Clay as already mentioned comes from Devon and Dorset, and is so called because it is cut out of the ground, sometimes from underground workings, in large lumps, or 'balls'. It is greyish brown when dug, but it fires to a much paler colour.

China Clay, or Kaolin, is mined in the Truro area by high pressure jets of water which wash the fine white clay out of the ground. Impurities are removed by filters and magnets, and then the excess water is spun out using centrifuges before transportation.

China Stone is also found in Cornwall, near to St. Austell, and is a variety of granite. Before use it has to be crushed to a powder, and defluorinated with water.

Flint is used as an additive in the mix because it both whitens and strengthens the finished product. It too has to be brought in from away – in this case from the south east and East Anglia where it is found as layers in deposits of chalk. Before it can be used in pottery making it is burnt in upright, gas-fired chambers, and then crushed between moving steel plates. Finally it is ground to a fine powder in a ball mill – a rotating horizontal cylinder lined with hard stone, and filled with unburnt flint pebbles and water. This grinding process takes up to a day to complete.

When the four basic ingredients have been assembled they are each reduced to a liquid form in a 'blunger' or mixing chamber where rotating paddles break down the clays, and mix them with water to produce 'slip', a creamy liquid. These four slips are then mixed together in a further chamber before passing to a storage and settlement vessel. After settlement the raw slip is de-watered by squeezing out the water under pressure to leave the 'body' or final earthenware mix in slabs. It is from these slabs that clay can be taken direct for throwing or modelling – or in the case of our vase, to be remixed with water to make a final 'slip' for casting.

The Modeller – important and well paid

Although bowls, cups and saucers would be made by partly automated methods direct from the clay 'body', the majority of Carlton Ware pieces were made by the process of 'Slip-Casting' using moulds. Before this could happen several stages had to be completed. Each one of the well known Carlton shapes had first to be created by one of the most important and best paid people in the works – the Modeller. He (or she) had to carve the original shape from solid clay using the drawings provided by the factory designer. When the design had been created in three dimensional form it was fired, and then used to create a Master Block – the first mould in Plaster of Paris, probably in two, three or four parts. As shapes often stayed in use for many years, a plaster mould would be used over and over again, and because plaster is quite soft, gradual wear would result, with consequent loss of detail and sharpness of the end product. To avoid this the Master Block was only used to create a Master Case, or pristine clay example of the shape concerned. Working moulds in plaster would then be made from the Master Case, and these could be used 30 or 40 times before replacement.

Slip Casting

Once moulds were available production could start. Our vase uses a three part mould involving two halves and a base. This is strapped together, and liquid slip is poured in to fill the mould. As Plaster of Paris is very porous water is absorbed from the slip, and a layer of clay is deposited on the inside of the mould. If necessary the slip is topped up during this process, but after about an hour it is safe to pour the excess slip away, and carefully remove the 'green' vase from the mould. At this stage the vase is still soft, and can be easily damaged. It is placed on a shelf to dry for a day or so, and then it goes off for its biscuit firing.

The first, or 'Biscuit' firing is to remove all moisture from the clay, and to heat it to a temperature of some 1150°C, at which

Bowls, cups and saucers were not slip cast, but profiled on a turntable using a 'Jigger' as shown here. Note the ball of clay being flattened into a disc for the next saucer (in the foreground). Courtesy Coalport China Museum

The process of slip casting

1. The mould is typically in three pieces.
2. The mould is strapped together and slip (liquid clay) is poured in, and left to stand.
3. After an hour the excess liquid is poured away, and the mould can be opened to show the soft cast vase inside.
4. (left) Casting, still soft, straight from the mould; (middle) casting left overnight to dry and harden – note rough edges where there were joints in the mould (right) vase after Biscuit firing to harden and fettling to remove the rough edges. It is now ready for glazing and decoration.
Photo's courtesy Coalport China Museum

temperature chemical changes take place, and the clay's ingredients fuse together to become the hard, though porous substance known as 'biscuit'. For the first half of this century firing was carried out in the famous bottle kilns. As it was only economic to fire large numbers of items at once, the kilns were quite large; and the wares had to be protected from direct contact with the smoke and ash of the fires, as well as stacked to use all the available space.

The 'Saggar Maker's Bottom Knocker'

This was done using Saggars. These were round, lidless containers made from fireclay, and used to hold the green wares during the first, or biscuit firing. Each pottery employed their own Saggar making teams as several different sizes and shapes would be required, and a large Bottle kiln could hold as many as 3500 Saggars at once. Since each Saggar would only last for five or six firings replacements were constantly required. The gang consisted of a Filler, who batted out slabs of clay into a rectangular frame, and then sliced this into strips to form the sides of the Saggar. Next to him would be the interestingly named 'Saggar Maker's Bottom Knocker', often only a lad aged 11 or 12, responsible for

The Saggar Makers Workshop, note the 'Batter' or flat headed beater used to flatten out the clay. On the left is a turntable with a wooden mould, and the iron hoop used to frame the base or 'Bottom'. Courtesy Coalport China Museum

batting out a clay slab to an even thickness inside an iron hoop of slightly larger size than the base of the Saggar. Finally the Saggar Maker himself was the skilled man, responsible for forming the sides around a wooden drum, and then making a safe join between the base and the sides of the Saggar, which he did on a turntable. As Saggars could be stacked on top of one another 20 or 30 high in the kiln, faulty work by the Saggar Maker could be very costly indeed!

A single firing would use 10 to 15 tons of coal

Green wares were placed in the Saggars, with flat wares being bedded in layers of silver sand, and hollow wares such as our vase being located upside down in grooved plaster rings to minimise distortion during firing. Once put into the Saggars these would be loaded into the kiln by Placers, carrying the stacked Saggers on their heads. Rolled-up stockings made into a doughnut shape were put inside their caps to provide a flat base on which several Saggars could be balanced – and to reduce bruising! Once the kiln was full, perhaps with up to 40,000 individual pieces, the entrance door, or Clammins, would be bricked up except for a small inspection hole, and the furnaces spaced around the kiln at ground level would be lit.

The Biscuit firing would take temperatures inside the kiln to about 1150°C, and would take 50 to 60 hours to complete. During this time a single kiln would use between 10 and 15 tons of coal! As there were over 2000 Bottle Kilns in the Stoke area up to the Second World War the consumption of coal was vast – and the resultant smoke, dust and smog in the atmosphere were a real hazard to health. It was calculated that average life expectancy of a male pottery worker early in this century was just 46 years!

Although in this chapter we are looking at production of one of the famous 1930s pieces, we should not forget that production of superb bestwares as well as all of the rest of Carlton's range continued after the Second World War. Recognising the hazards to health as well as the high cost of fuelling the old, dirty Bottle Kilns, Cuthbert Wiltshaw and his fellow directors installed a modern electric Glost kiln in about 1946, and followed this with an electric Biscuit

'Placing' or loading the full Sagger into the kiln took strength and skill. kiln held up to 3500 Saggars. Courtes Gladstone Working Pottery Museum

The final stage

One of the hallmarks of Carlton's finest wares was, and is, the superlative effect achieved when top enamels are employed to give detail in colour over the glowing background of an underglaze foundation. The highly skilled team of paintresses used enamels made up from powdered metal oxides in very precise proportions. These were mixed into a soft paste, sometimes known as 'Egyptian Paste' with turpentine and fat oil on a glass palette. Exact recipes were required to ensure colour consistency, and these were jealously guarded by individual factories, but main ingredients included:

Iron	Reds, Rust, Browns
Copper	Green (in an oxidising atmosphere)
	Red (in a reducing atmosphere)
Cobalt	Blues
Tin	White, Bluish white
Uranium	Very bright Yellow
Antimony	Yellow
Manganese	Browns, Purples
Gold	Purple of Cassis
Chromium	Yellow
	plus Cobalt – Blue Green, Grey Green
	plus Tin – Pink, Crimson

The paintresses use a range of camel hair brushes of different profiles to add final touches of colour to the pattern, adding brightness to foliage, embroidery to the friezes and colourful depth to the featured design. After a final trip to the enamel oven our vase is

The finished article. A stunning pair of vases in the Bell pattern show off all the techniques and artistry of the Copeland Street works in the 1930s.

Up to 1945 there were over 2000 bottle kilns in the Stoke area. This group with their associated buildings are all that survive. They are at the Gladstone Working Pottery Museum. Courtesy Gladstone Working Pottery Museum

ready for inspection, its long and complex path through the processes at Copeland Street are over.

With such diverse and varied skills contributing to its finished form it is perhaps small wonder that today we eagerly seek out, collect and cherish the truly beautiful works of art that are Carlton Ware.

Carlton China – and W & R's Crested Ware

Wiltshaw and Robinson entered the crested china market around 1901 or 1902, when the company was only some twelve years old. They had clearly been successful in their early years, and were eager not to be left out of an established and fast growing sector of the market. Although competing head on with Shelley, Arcadian and market leader Goss, once again quality served the company well, and the W & R crown mark was to appear on crested china for some twenty-five years.

The Manufacture of Heraldic China

Heraldic or Crested Wares are often described as 'Bone China', but this is usually inaccurate terminology. Most of such wares were made from parian, a variety of soft paste porcelain whose ingredients were Kaolin, or China Clay, China Stone (a variety of granite) and Felspar, naturally occurring rock containing Aluminium Silicates. Parian took moulded detail well, and had the virtue of bonding closely with its glaze, so that crazing and cracking of the glaze is rare in parian wares. In addition parian was considerably cheaper to make than bone china, lacking the expense of imported bone. Like bone china it can be cast to give thin walled items which show off the translucent quality of the material, but unlike bone china it is of a slightly greyish tinge after firing, contrasting with the delicate pure white hue bone china possesses.

To give the Souvenir pieces their identity, the crest, or coat of arms of the town had to be applied, and this was a two stage process. The black outline was applied to the plain body of the piece as a lithographic transfer, either before or more commonly after glazing. The details were then hand painted using the finest camel hair brushes, and employing both opaque and transparent enamels. The latter were used over particularly fine detail in the outline transfer, such as small foliage, so that this detail was not lost. Where possible, however, thicker, opaque paints in bright colours picked out the quarters of the coats of arms and other features of each crest. The close study of the finest of these heraldic pieces reveals miniature masterpieces of precision painting. If the pattern called for it, gilding for edging and other parts would also be hand applied. When enamelling was complete the pieces were fired at a low temperature to bond the decoration to the porcelain, thus ensuring the survival of these tiny crests and mottos in good order right up to the present day.

Although our interest in this book is centred on the output of the Copeland Street works of Wiltshaw and Robinson, we cannot review the history and features of Heraldic, or crested china without setting Wiltshaw & Robinson's production in its context. That context can be considered under two headings:

Heraldic pieces with specific connections, Anvil from Gretna Green (£14-£18/$25-$30); Bandstand from Southend-on-Sea (£40-£48/$70-$90); Bishop's Mitre from York (£16-£20/$30-$35).

the social environment of the times, and the pioneering work in this specialised field of William Henry Goss.

W.H.Goss and Heraldic China
Although Wiltshaw and Robinson, under the trade mark of 'Carlton China' made crested china of delicate and collectable quality for over twenty years, they were not the first to do so; and many of the ground rules for both design and distribution had already been drawn up by the Goss company by the time that Carlton China appeared. W.H. Goss had worked as a designer for Copeland during the 1850s, until leaving in 1858 to set up in his own right with a gentleman called Peake. They produced pottery in local clays, or terra cotta, but became known over the next ten years principally as 'parian china manufacturers'. In 1868 the partnership split up, and Goss formed his own company producing a range of quality wares in porcelain and terra cotta as well as parian. Goss had experimented with small quantities of Heraldic items in his earlier years, producing these for university colleges and public schools, and in the early 1880s he conceived the idea *of producing the arms of every town, etc., in Great Britain, and publishing the same on some antique model from an original in that town*. It was his strict idea that these items would only be available from one agent per town, and would only be offered for sale in the town whose coat of arms they bore.

These very strict limitations were relaxed in due course as popular demand for the affordable presents and souvenirs increased; thus any given shape might be produced with several different crests, though stockists were only permitted to sell items bearing their own town's coat of arms. So great was the public enthusiasm that in 1900 the first *Goss Record* was published by J. J. Jarvis of Enfield, listing all of the 500 or so stockists and all of the coats of arms that they sold. The heraldic china also appealed to collectors of limited means, and in 1904 the 'League of Goss Collectors' was founded to encourage interest in heraldry, and provide a forum for competitions and exchange of pieces among collectors. The League lasted into the early 1920s, becoming the 'International League of Goss Collectors' in 1918.

The social environment
As can be seen, by the turn of the century, when Wiltshaw and Robinson decided to join in the production of Heraldic china, a great deal of the initial work had been done. The market identified by Goss was growing rapidly, and no doubt a significant influence on popular demand was the growth in rail travel for the masses. The expansion of the rail network, coupled with the rising affluence of ordinary working people as a result of the industrial revolution, brought about the 'day trip', and the seaside holiday on an unprecedented scale. Then, as now, there was a natural interest in bringing home a souvenir of the trip, and items of Heraldic China were tailor made as suitable souvenirs being small, affordable, and identified with the place visited by means of the coat of arms they bore.

Carlton China joins in
Against this background, the Carlton works launched its own range of Souvenir China around 1902. There is no record available of the full range of items produced, or of any Club for W & R collectors, if one ever existed. Indeed, although the early Carlton China pieces followed the established Goss practice of being modelled upon historic artefacts

Earliest items were reproductions of historical artefacts, (from left) Old Swedish Kettle (£7-£9/$12-$15); York Roman Ewer (£7-£9/$12-$15; Roman Pot from Merthyr Tydfil (£7-£9/$12-$15), Portland Vase (£7-£9/$12-$15); Hastings Kettle (£7-£9/$12-£15).

from the outset the pieces seem to have been marked with a variety of crests to suit the towns from which orders were received. Hence it is possible to find identical pieces in Carlton China bearing several different town coats of arms.

The earliest designs

As already described, Wiltshaw & Robinson followed the established practice of producing miniature reproductions of genuine historical artefacts. These are dignified by having a legend printed on the base stating upon what the piece is modelled, thus: *'Roman Ewer from original Inhospitium found at York'* (No. 178) and *'Model of Ancient Kettle dredged up near Hastings. In Hastings Museum'* (No. 166). That W & R did not restrict the use of such reproductions to the locality in which the original discovery was made is evinced by the crests borne by these two pieces in our collection. These are St. Pancras and Spalding respectively!

Soon, however, Carlton China began to diversify, and as the prosperous Edwardians went on their day trips, and enjoyed some of the new technical innovations such as the motor car and the gramophone, more complex crested items were introduced featuring both these advances, and the general feeling of light heartedness and good fortune which

Souvenirs reflected technical advances, sewing machine (£30-£36/$50-$65); gramophone (£38-£45/$70-$85); motor scooter (£60-£70/£$000-$000); charabanc (£52-£58/$95-$115).

115

prevailed. The very early charabanc shown in the accompanying photograph has the legend 'Over the Hills and Far Away' cheerfully emblazoned across the back.

Souvenirs of wartime . . .

The mood was to change to a more sombre one, however, with the onset of the First World War. This had two consequences on the ranges of crested china produced by the various manufacturers, as the Tommies were keen to have items available with regimental crests, and even with the crests of French towns on them, while the general public bought items with military connotations, Battleships and Tanks, Ambulances and Shells. In addition the rather poignant message on the cooking range in the photograph is clearly of wartime origin: 'Keep the Home Fires burning till the Boys come Home'.

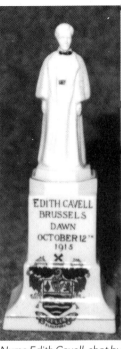

Many items were made reflecting the Great War. Coal scuttle (in shape of German helmet (£6-£8/$00-$00); ambulance (£35-£45/ $60-$80); Range (Keep the Home Fires Burning) (£22-£28/$40-$50); field gun (£21-£27/$40-$50); battleship (£90-£110/$170-$200).

Nurse Edith Cavell, shot by the Germans in 1915. Statue (£28-£35/$50-$65).

. . . and of the peace that followed

As the country breathed sighs of relief after the war the preferred pieces in souvenir ware changed yet again. Domestic items, farm animals, romantic and Good Luck charms became the order of the day. The use of metallic salts to create lustre glazes had been discovered, and some of Carlton's items were given a mother of pearl lustrous finish. The traditional hand enamelled coats of arms were supplemented by the use of pictorial transfers depicting particular views of some resorts, and of course 'Lucky White Heather' was a continuing favourite. Whether these later developments represent a decline in quality, as some may think, or

Reminders of holidays by the sea. Whelk shells (£7-£9/$12-$15), Valise (£12-£18/$20-$30), Lighthouse (£16-£22/$30-$40), Life boat (£15-£20/$25-$35).

whether tastes were simply changing, it is a fact that demand for Heraldic china declined during the 1920s. The Goss factory was finally sold on the verge of bankruptcy in 1928, while Wiltshaw and Robinson, who were not so dependant on the souvenir market, had been busy developing innovative table wares and the sumptuous lustre finishes which were to play such a part in the next chapter in their history.

Novelty items included farm animals, hen sitting (£12-£16/$20-$30). cat (£12-£16/$20-$30); chick hatching (£11-£15/$20-$30); Pig (£18-£22/$30-$40).

Homely sentiments often appeared on souvenirs. These items all have a 'Good Luck' element. Note that the Swastika was a good luck sign early this century! Shamrock dish (£4-£6/$6-$10); Sundial (£25-£28/$45-$50); Lucky White Heather (£5-£7/$8-$12); Good Luck Armchair (£36-£42/$65-$80).

Fruit and Floral Embossed Wares

Desirable for over 60 years

Of all the many and varied ceramic forms which were produced at the Copeland Street Works, it is probable that the embossed patterns featuring a long sequence of fruit and floral designs are the most widely collected in Britain, and across the world. The reasons are not hard to find: from their earliest days the buying public liked the combination of reasonable price and attractive, clear detail in the modelling. The appeal to today's collectors is still the same, but with the added delight of knowing that the variety to be sought, both in shape and in the many diverse patterns, is almost limitless. A group of these embossed wares in almost any pattern always looks charming, and prices for most pieces are still well within the pockets of many collectors, as they cover a range from £15 for a small dish to £150 for a tall jug, or a large handled basket.

Prices have changed, however. Trade advertisements from the late 1930s offer a choice of boxed sets containing a small jam dish plus spoon or knife of such patterns as Tulip, Blackberry, Daisy and Buttercup for eleven shillings and ninepence per dozen! In present day money this equates to just under five pence per boxed set, whereas most collectors today would be pleased to pay £30 to £40 for the same item!

Decorative – or for daily use?

Of course, today we would only purchase these pieces for display, and there is some disagreement about whether the floral embossed wares were originally made to be merely decorative, or to be used on a daily basis. Perhaps practical considerations provide the best answers to this debate. There is no doubt that a jug in Foxglove or Apple Blossom can be used for pouring water, milk or lemonade, or that a bon bon dish can be placed upon the sideboard full of sweets to tempt the passer by. But consider the practicality of cutting your toast into soldiers on a Foxglove plate. The very detail in the moulding, the clear, serrated edges to the leaves which makes the plate so attractive render it anything but practical in everyday use. The glaze on all the raised pieces of the pattern would quickly be ruined, and if many of these pieces had been used in daily life we would surely be presented with a stream of scratched and chipped items today.

As a second consideration, Carlton produced more than thirty embossed patterns between 1930 and 1960, and while a number of these, such as Apple Blossom, Foxglove and the later Convolvulus were made in a full range of pieces for the table, many were not. Indeed some of the patterns were only ever made in one or two shapes – surely intended as an attractive display on the dresser, rather than to be bought for everyday use.

Origins and early patterns

As discussed above, the embossed wares became primarily decorative in their appeal, but developed from some ideas explored by the factory during the 1920s. In about 1925 the first of the 'Salad Wares' appeared, with strongly modelled, red painted crabs and lobsters supporting dishes in the shape of lettuce leaves. The first series was titled Crab and Lobster by the factory. This specialised range was followed during the next couple of years by some pretty tableware ranges which were finished with a mother of pearl lustre, and which bore shallow, embossed oranges and peaches. These were genuine table items, and sadly not many have survived. A set together would still make a fetching display. Another of these pearlised ranges showed a perimeter of moulded clam shells set on a 'coral' base.

In the early 1930s multicoloured patterns such as Fruit Basket (1932) and Rock Garden (1934/5), (commonly referred to as Garden Wall), made their bow, and during the same period the bigger, bolder designs of Oak and Anemone appeared. A second Salad series christened 'Lettuce' was introduced in about 1935, about a year ahead of the first of the really popular floral ranges, Buttercup, followed by Tulip (made for the table), Daisy and Blackberry. A much fuller list of these patterns can be found in the chapter on Dating, but it would be remiss not to mention here three of the all-time best sellers, all of them made in a wide variety of shapes: Wild Rose which started to appear in 1937, Apple Blossom (1938-40), and Foxglove (1940 onwards). No other ranges approached these for popularity, as is evidenced by the quantities of these patterns still available at Fairs today. Indeed, such was the appeal of Apple Blossom that it was reissued in a revised form, as part of the Arthur Woods attempt to revive Carlton Ware in the mid 1970s. However, from the success of Foxglove in the 1940s, it was to be almost twenty years before the new Magnolia and Convolvulus ranges of 1958 to 1960 were produced in similar volume and scope.

The Australian dimension
Collectors are often puzzled, and, sad to say, are often misled by dealers about the significance of the common Carlton Ware Backstamps which read :

Carlton Ware
MADE IN ENGLAND
'TRADE MARK'
REGISTERED AUSTRALIAN DESIGN

Sometimes the words, 'REGISTRATION APPLIED FOR' also appear. We have heard it said that these words signify that the pattern was designed for the Australian market – we have even been told, as a great secret, that all the plants on designs so marked are Australian plants, (Apple Blossom? Tulip?). In fact, these words relate to efforts made by Wiltshaw and Robinson to prevent their designs being copied by the Japanese. A great deal of Carlton Ware as well as pottery from other British factories was being exported to Australia before the Second World War, and in the 1930s the Japanese became adept at making accurate copies for sale at very low prices. Placards reading 'COPIES OF FAMOUS DESIGNS – 1ST QUALITY CHINA – 18 PIECES 5/11' (29.5p) could be seen in shop windows, and these copies obviously hurt trade for legitimate importers as well as for the British manufacturers. While Britain had no direct means of redress for this, Australia did have a treaty with the Japanese through the South East Asia Treaty Organisation (SEATO), which prohibited copying of any design actually registered in Australia, and marked as such. In negotiations, the Australian Association of British Manufacturers persuaded the Registration Authorities to re-examine the procedure and costs for getting a design registered. In consequence the requirement for a design to obtain registration was altered from twelve photographs to two, and the fee was reduced from one pound to five shillings.

As a result, Carlton, amongst other manufacturers, were able to keep their antipodean markets by registering many of their popular designs. This brought into use the two variants of the Backstamp referred to above, which went on all production of certain ranges from 1935 right through to about 1961. By this time the 'Registered Australian Design' mark was being applied to designs such as Pinstripe and Windswept which were only invented in 1958, long after the Japanese had ceased, at least for a time, to be any kind of threat.

The effect of the war

Once war had been declared in 1939, restrictions on the production of luxury goods were progressively introduced in the UK. Costly materials such as gold were severely rationed, and skilled craftsmen and women were needed for producing Spitfires and armaments rather than for handpainted vases. Factories could only obtain very limited permits for such goods for valued export orders. Whether for this reason or not, we can say for certain that several of the new Floral Embossed patterns devised around 1939 to 1940 were only ever produced as a single shape, or possibly two or three, and much if not all of the production was sent abroad. Thus items like Campion (1771), Begonia (1768) and Pyrethrum (1751) are to be found in New Zealand and Australia, but scarcely appear in the UK except after making the round trip!

The wartime restrictions had a major impact on production of the embossed wares, but some production, even for the home market, did continue. However, with expensive glazes and handpainting both restricted, items for the home market had to be turned out in utility form, and so the keen eyed collector of today will, from time to time, spot pieces of familiar patterns – but with no decoration, and glazed in pale yellow or a rather washed out green. All the details of the mould are there, but none of the colour. These utility ranges also found an export market, as they were not only cheaper to buy, but avoided duty in some markets. It is, perhaps, of interest to keep one or two of these wartime pieces in a collection, as they are very much part of our history, as well as part of the story of Carlton Ware.

Fifties boldness

After the war, some of the established and successful designs continued in production, and were gradually replaced by a new set of floral embossed designs. Where the best designs of the 1930s had created whole plates and bowls in the form of overlapping leaves, with clusters of fruit and flowers to give colour, the 1950s patterns tended to feature boldly moulded fruit and flowers around the borders of smooth glazed bowls and dishes. Patterns included Poppy, new Daisy, Hydrangea, Vine and Grape, and these pieces were capable of practical use in the home. Platters, Hors d'oeuvres dishes and fruit bowls survive in reasonable numbers, and are rightly prized today.

Manufacture of the embossed wares always entailed extra expense, and by the early 1960s recessionary pressures were biting everywhere. For Carlton Ware Ltd. the golden era was over, and the twin embossed ranges of Magnolia and Convolvulus were the final entrants in a procession which had lasted over thirty-five years.

Records and Insurance

The importance of good records

Although they may not immediately be obvious there are a number of cogent reasons why you should keep quite detailed records about your acquisitions. Right from the start it is sensible to organise a book into columns into which you can enter details of each individual piece. Suggested headings would include:

Date of Purchase
Description of Piece (include colour, pattern and condition)
Measurements (Height and/or diameter)
Identification Marks (Impressed or Shape Number, Pattern Number etc)
Where bought and from whom
Asking Price
Actual Price Paid
Date Sold
To whom sold
Price realised

Photographs will be invaluable . .

By keeping these details carefully you will be able to see at a glance how many pieces you own – and just how much you have invested! These records will also be important if you ever have to justify a claim for damage or theft to your insurance company – but do not rely on written records alone if your collection is of any significant value. Take clear colour photographs of all new pieces, and keep them safe. If disaster strikes they will be invaluable.

It may seem strange to include columns for possible disposal, but most collectors find that, sooner or later, they want to sell off some earlier purchases. It may be that the initial collection proved to be a bit too diverse – after all very few people can contemplate collecting every type and range ever produced by Carlton Ware. As the collection develops you may wish to concentrate on certain periods, or particular colours – and let go of items which no longer fit in. It may be that, as is the case for most of us, you have budgetary constraints – in other words there are limits to what you can afford. In these circumstances you may wish to sell a few less important pieces to finance future purchases in your favourite range. It may be that you are simply running out of space!

For whatever reason it is important to keep track of what you sell, both so that you can compare selling prices with your original purchase price, and so that your record clearly shows what pieces you still possess, and what pieces you do not. We all think we have good memories – but pause for a minute, shut your eyes, and try to list all of your 45 pieces – or all 80 – or all 200! You will see the importance of a written record!

Insuring your collection

The steps you take to insure your collection are, of course, personal, but Carlton Ware is steadily increasing in value – partly because no more is being made, partly because it is increasingly appreciated by greater numbers of collectors, and partly because a quantity is inevitably lost every year through breakages. Whether you are able to insure your collection satisfactorily within your existing household Contents policy, or whether it seems best to arrange a separate policy, Insurance is essential to protect your interests – and must include cover both for Accidental Damage and Theft.

Review on a regular basis

Even quite small collections can have a value of a few hundreds of pounds, and it takes surprisingly few of the more highly decorated items to amount to a few thousand. So adequate insurance is vital, and you should make it a priority, not only to insure at the beginning, but to use your records to review your insured value on a regular basis – say every six months.

As a first step talk to your Household Contents insurer. Companies vary greatly in their attitudes to ceramic collections. Some will simply refuse to insure your contents if a collection is included, and you then have a choice of adding a separate policy or changing insurers. Other companies will insist that your contents value is suitably increased to cover the required amount, and will not require any other details unless any single piece exceeds a particular limit – usually £1000. Ceramics are not usually described as valuables in the way that jewelry and paintings are – but you should not take this for granted. Some insurers will accept your collection as a separate item, but only up to a certain value – always check if this is the case.

Many insurance companies take a helpful line over ceramics so that you can achieve cover within your household policy – and if your present company is not among these it may be worth thinking about a change to avoid excessive expense.

In the event of a claim . .

If you are unfortunate enough to have to claim as a result of breakages:

1. Take photographs of the broken pieces – and do **not** throw the bits away. There are dodgy people about who will try things on, even among collectors, and your insurer is entitled to see the evidence.

2. In addition to your purchase records ask a reputable dealer to give you a written valuation for the damaged pieces. This will support your claim, especially if some time has elapsed since you bought the pieces, and they have increased in value.

3. Do not forget that the value of what was a complete coffee or tea set may well be reduced by breakage of one or more items, and this reduction should form part of your claim as well as the value of the broken pieces.

For two last thoughts on this subject; firstly do make sure you have Accidental Damage cover at least on your Contents insurance; and finally – do not drop your precious Carlton Ware. Have an accident with a pushchair, vacuum cleaner or dog, but do not simply drop it. Such an act is regarded as negligence, not an accident, and you will not be covered!

A Carlton Ware Pattern List

One of the most tantalising aspects of Carlton Ware is that, with some five different owners from 1967 to the present, and at least two periods when it was believed that production had ceased for ever, vital historical information has been lost, thrown away or possibly misappropriated. Today the whereabouts of only two of the original Shape Books is known – these, along with two Pattern Books which probably originate from Birks and Rawlins, are currently being cared for on loan at the Potteries Museum and Art Gallery, Stoke-on-Trent.

One of the vital Carlton Ware Pattern books, thought to contain many of the original illustrations of the designs of the 1930s, was also in the Museum at Stoke until 1989, when it was taken away by Mr. McCluskey of Grosvenor Ceramics, the then owner of Carlton Ware. Sadly he did not return it, and the current whereabouts of this priceless piece of history is not known. It seems unlikely that such a large and distinctive item was merely mislaid – and in all probability it now resides with someone with a commercial interest in keeping it to themselves. Wheresoever this book may be, no complete catalogue of Carlton Ware production is available, and the would be collector must play detective to identify patterns and dates to the best of his, or her ability.

The Pattern List below will help with this task. It has been compiled over time from many sources, from friends on scraps of paper, by word of mouth and by telephone, by reading, by attendance at auctions and most of all by the kind cooperation of many, many dealers and collectors in allowing me to upturn their prized possessions to read their numbers, and record their appearance. The list is not complete – and probably never will be; it almost certainly contains some errors.

Some Pattern numbers are difficult to read – and sometimes contradictions occur because a busy painter on a production line simply applied the wrong number. In the early years of Blush Ware production many items were not numbered, and after the Second World War the practice of numbering individual pieces was virtually abandoned. In addition it seems certain that many Patterns were drawn up (and numbered) which never saw final production. Therefore the list below cannot be perfect. I offer my thanks to all those who have assisted in its compilation, and my apologies for any errors which may be found.

Many frequently seen patterns from the post-war period have no known pattern number, and some of these occur in many different colourways. It would be pointless to list endless un-numbered designs, but some of the colourways relating to later production of the New Mikado pattern are listed as an example.

When it comes to names, there are quite a number of the well known Carlton designs which have an original Factory name, and these are shown in bold type. Over the years many other patterns have been called by various names which dealers and collectors have felt suited them, and which made referring to the various patterns a lot easier than

123

trying to remember numbers. Many such names in popular usage have been recorded in italic type in the list below.

In order to further our collective knowledge, work on this list continues – and information which corrects or adds to it will be welcomed by the author and the publisher for inclusion in future editions of this book.

Pattern Number	Description and Name
523	Long Tailed Bird
524	Matt black ground with exotic bird on bough of flowering tree, all pattern in white outlined in gilt.
528	Matt black ground with natural looking sprays of red roses and leaves. **Red Rose**
595	Matt black ground with bird on a bough of a flowering tree – leaves in green, peony-like blossoms in pink, all outlined in gilt.
603	Pale green ground with white perimeter band
604	Pale green ground with dark friezes 'Sprigged-Ware', with white classical figures in raised relief
614	Dark green ground in matt glaze with frieze of white foliage and pattern of white dancing figures in classical style, both applied as sprigs forming raised relief in the manner of Wedgwood.
624	Complex design where matt black ground is overlaid with skeletal plant figures in deep blue, the whole separated into zones by dividing bands in white with an overlay of leaves. Main zones contain large cartouches of white ground with colourful posies of flowers. **Reproduction Swansea China**
722	Matt green ground with inset flowers and leaves in underglaze enamels, with gilt edging. White stork in enamel. 'Cloisonne Ware'
723	Matt black ground with inset flowers and leaves in underglaze enamels with gilt edging. White Stork in enamel. 'Cloissonne Ware'
1089	Blushware. White ground, shading to light caramel, with pattern of life-like Chrysanthemums in beige and orange with green leaves. **Chrysanthemum**
1162	Blushware. Vellum ground, shading to warm brown, border in high glaze deep cobalt blue, with centre pattern showing handpainted flowers in red, pink and yellow. **Cornucopia**
1230	Blushware. White ground with brown and grey figures.
1304	Green/red. Flower
B1509	Blushware pattern with pale beige ground blushing to butterscotch brown, with gilt rim and feet, and naturalistic spray of flowers (poppies or Chrysanthemums) in shades of brown.
1655	White ground, with pattern of flowers in dark cobalt blue outlined in gilt, and further bright red enamelled poppy-like flowers, lavishly surrounded in gilt.
1732	Floral sprays printed in colours
1883(?)	**Mikado** (see 2364)
1981	Blue ground, with decorations in enamels and raised gilt of sprays of Carnations.
1987	White ground with copious pattern of cobalt blue flowers underglaze, with profuse gilding providing a surround as well as outlining the flowers. **Petunia**
2006	Black ground with coloured and gilt dragons
2021	Blue ground with pagodas and foliage, some fern-like. one pagoda with ornamental wall, another with post/rail fence. Frieze with oriental motifs and rectangular lines. **Kang Hsi**
2030	Matt black ground with pink and green blossom sprays. **Peach Blossom**
2031	Pink ground, birds on prunus blossom, chrysanthemums and good luck symbols. **Kien Lung**
2041(?)	As 2071 below.
2053	Terra cotta/Black. **Kien Lung**
2071	Royal blue ground with sprays of ornate flowers growing into the air from rockery on which Pheasant is standing. Colours and gilt. **Pheasant and Rockery**
2088	White ground. Child's Flowers
2091	Matt black ground with trailing stems of Wisteria in shades of pink and green. **Old Wisteria**
2095	Pinky red 'Armand' lustre ground, with life-like pictures of moths and butterflies in underglaze enamels with gilt outlines. **Flies**
2097A(?)	Royal blue ground, otherwise as 2907/8, **Magpies**
2099	Pinky red 'Armand' lustre ground, as 2095 above. **Flies**
2112	Dark green 'ARMAND' lustre ground with pattern of lifelike butterflies. **Flies**
2115	Matt black ground, with cartouches of birds of paradise among foliage radiating through yellow segments from a central medallion of flowers. Colours and gilt.
2126	White ground with a bird among flowers and foliage in oriental style, the rim with cartouches of flowers the whole printed and painted in colours and gilt
—	Blue glazed ground, with pair of 'Fabulous Birds', white birds with long tails perching in peony trees
2128	Powder blue ground with oriental scenes

2131	Mottled orange/yellow lustre ground, otherwise as 2134. **Flies**
2134	Pale blue 'ARMAND' lustre ground with pattern of lifelike butterflies. **Flies**
2144	Matt blue ground with irregular self coloured spots, with birch-like trees with black and white trunks, and exotic pendant foliage in colours and gilt. **Forest Tree**
2151	Blue background with ornate but formal basket of flowers in red, pink, yellow and blue enamels and gilt. *Basket of Flowers*
2175	Matt black ground with large terra cotta panels containing inner, black cartouches with crested birds among foliage, enamelled in mauve, orange, blue and white. **Worcester Birds**
2178	Dancing figures
2184	Matt black ground otherwise as 2151. (also found in blue). *Basket of Flowers*
2189	As 2151. *Basket of Flowers*
2195	Matt black ground covered in gilt tracery, with large blue panels containing inner, black cartouches with crested birds among foliage, enamelled in mauve, orange, blue and white. **Worcester Birds**
2196	**Worcester Birds.** See also 2175
2199	**Mikado** (see 2364)
2215	Blush ware. **Wild Rose**
2216	Blue ground with oriental scene of figures in temple. (see 2481, ?Temple)
2221	Matt black ground with yellow diamond shaped cartouches containing pictures of birds. *?Bird and Chequered Border*
2238	Black ground, divided into vertical panels by white, decorated stripes, pendant sprays of wisteria blossom. **Old Wisteria**
2250	Blue ground with cockerell and flowers. **Cockerells**
2270	Matt black ground, oriental couple among pagodas and terraces, painted with full colours to landscape and garments in the style of 'Chinaland', with 'Kissing Birds' in flight. **Mikado**
2281	Matt black ground with cockerell and flowers. **Cockerells**
2355	Pearly, light blue mottled ground with Chinoiserie design of pagodas and bridges, with pair of 'kissing birds' in flight above, colours and gilt all underglaze. **Mikado**
2359	Powder blue ground, Chinoiserie pagodas and bridges with oriental ladies. Matt finish.
2364	Powder blue ground, oriental ladies among pagodas, and bridges with pair of 'kissing' birds in flight above, the pattern is outlined in gilt and painted in bright coloured, overglaze enamels. **Mikado**
2389	Butterfly
2399	Blue lustre ground with pagodas and bridges in gilt only. **Mikado**
2405	**Cock and Peony Spray**
2412	Pale yellow ground with illustration of bird perching on spray of prunus blossom. **?Prunus and Bird**
2420	Blue Armand lustre ground with pattern of butterflies in underglaze colours. **Flies**
2428	Deep blue lustre ground, Chinoiserie figures, pagodas, bridges.
2431	Bright yellow ground with illustration of bird perching on a spray of prunus blossom. **?Prunus and Bird**
2432	Royal blue lustre ground, with two cranes in pool, one drinking, beside two stems of bamboo. **Stork and Bamboo**
2437	Powder blue ground, (also found in dark blue), naturalistic fish in underglaze enamels, with on-glaze gilt outlines and strands of seaweed. **Fish and Seaweed**
2440	Lemon yellow ground. **Fish and Seaweed**
2441	Rich Pink ground with pair of fish (like catfish) in blue/purple swimming together among gilt seaweed. **Fish and Seaweed**
2463	Yellow ground with sprays of Prunus blossom both open and in bud in shades of white and pink. **New Prunus Spray**
2466	White ground with blue border, with illustration of tree with dark blue trunk, birds and red flowers. *Bird and Tree Peony*
2470	Matt black ground, Chinoiserie figures, pagodas and bridges.
2481	Blue high glaze ground, with oriental scenes depicting a pagoda with a large circular doorway, figures and hillocks in colours and gilt. **Temple**
2482	Deep blue lustre ground, Chinoiserie as 2481, but in gilt only. **Temple**
2519	Blue ground, Chinoiserie in gilt and colours depicting pagodas, causeway, bridges and figure on punt-like boat. **Barge**
2530	Pearly lustre on white ground with realistic Kingfisher sitting on branch over a river. Other branches above. **Kingfisher**
2644	Colours with geometric motif, for coffee set
2706	Pearl white ground with Egyptian motifs and cartouches in underglaze colours and gilt. Often with black frieze. **Tutankhamun**
2708	Matt black ground with Egyptian motifs in gilt only. **Tutankhamun**
2709(?)	Matt black ground with Egyptian motifs in colours and gilt. **Tutankhamun**
2710	Powder blue ground with Egyptian motifs in colours and gilt. **Tutankhamun**
2711	Royal blue ground with Egyptian motifs in colours and gilt. **Tutankhamun**

2721	Yellow lustre ground with black edging and no gilding, featuring sprays comprising black twigs and white orange blossom, with one small bird in mainly orange enamel.
2722	Orange lustre exterior (with pearl lustre white interior), decorated with sprays comprising black twigs and white orange blossom
2728	Deep blue ground, Chinoiserie pagodas and bridges and trees in colours and gilt. Probably the most common Chinoiserie pattern, also on rouge. **New Mikado**
2729	Blue ground, pattern as 2728 above, but often in gilt only. **New Mikado**
2755(?)	As 2355. **Mikado**
2757	Speckled pink ground
2779	White ground with yellow border and black painted edges. Pattern of spray of handpainted flowers within black transfer printed outlines.
2810	Matt black ground, with emerald green frieze containing oriental motifs, main ground decorated with Chinoiserie pattern in colours and gilt.
2814	Royal blue lustre ground, with pagodas and bridges in gilt and under-glaze colours of red and green, as well as overglaze enamels. **New Mikado**
2818	Deep red ground, with ferocious dragon in black and gilt, among black and gilt clouds. **Dragon and Cloud**
2822	Deep blue ground, storks in a garden scene. **Stork and Bamboo**
2825	Red lustre ground with oriental ladies, pagodas and bridges in gilt only. (see 2728). **New Mikado**
—	Blue lustre ground with naturalistic sprays of twigs with Prunus blossom and foliage, and perching bird **Prunus and Bird**.
2831	White ground with multicoloured border/frieze, naturalistic sprays of twigs with Prunus blossom and foliage, and perching bird in blue and yellow. **Prunus and Bird**
2854	Powder blue ground, with Chinoiserie scene, pagodas, two figures on a bridge, pair of love birds in flight, all in black and gilt, for tea service.
2857	Blue lustre ground, with birds and prunus blossom in colours and gilt in chinoiserie style. **Prunus and Bird**
2863	**Cameo**
2867	**Cameo**
2869	Orange ground. **Cameo**
2880	Terra cotta ground with black lower band, Chinoiserie pattern as 2481, and with medallions of oriental scenes on black lower border. **Temple**
2881	Matt black ground, terra cotta frieze with Chinoiserie pagodas and bridges, with pair of 'kissing birds' in flight. **Mikado**
2882	Blue ground. **Persian**
2883	Blue ground. **Persian**
2884	Royal blue ground, Persian design of figures in a temple, with prayermat in front, surrounded by palm trees and desert landscape. **Persian**
2885	Royal blue lustre ground, Persian design in colours and gilt. **Persian**
2886	Blue ground with mixed sprays of Oranges, Cherries and other fruits in orange, red and white. **Orchard**
2903	Blue ground, with black and gold oriental dragon among stylised small clouds. **Dragon and Cloud**
2905	White ground with lower half painted in red, top half with figures of nymphs dancing round. **?Dancing Figures**
2907	Tomato red ground with black and white friezes, magpies perching on branches, and flying. **Magpies**
2907A	As 2907 above, but with blue ground. **Magpies**
2908	As 2907 above, but with yellow ground. **Magpies**
2909	Dark Blue ground with pendulous round peach-like fruit hanging on branch with slender leaves, all outlined in gilt with subtle underglaze colours. *Fruit Bough*
2910	Matt black ground with Chinoiserie pattern of pagodas and bridges in green and gilt. **Mikado**
2911	As 2908 above, tomato red ground. **Magpies**
2913	Matt black ground with pale yellow top frieze ornamented with Chinoiserie pictures. Main decoration is gnarled oriental tree trunk with perched game bird with small red crest. **Cretonne**
2914	Black ground with jade green banding, heavily decorated with gilt oriental scenes
2917	Matt black exterior, vivid orange lustre interior, for coffee and tea sets.
2922	Matt black and orange lustre exterior with gilt and enamel frieze (coffee set)
2928	Yellow ground, with chinoiserie pattern as 2481 in gilt and enamels of black, green, red and blue. Border with band of cartouches of oriental scenes. **Temple**
2929	Powder blue ground, matt finish, Chinoiserie pagodas and bridges in pattern as 2481 above. **Temple**
2932	Royal blue lustre ground, with two white cranes, one drinking from a pool, the other standing on one foot. (See 2432). **Stork and Bamboo**
2933	Orange ground. **Stork and Bamboo**
2936	Blue ground, with figures in pagoda grounds. **Chinese Tea Garden**
2940	White ground with orange lustre upper frieze, and pearl lustre interior.
2941	Green ground with black lower band. Chinoiserie pattern as 2481. **Temple**
2944	Matt black ground with orange lustre frieze with gilt and colour decoration. Central orange medallion showing two silhouetted figures playing with bubbles. *Moonlight Cameo*

2946	Orange ground with white central medallion showing two silhouetted children playing with bubbles. *Moonlight Cameo*
2948	Orange ground. Complex Chinoiserie design with pagodas, bridges, boats and figures against landscape in natural underglaze colours. **Chinaland**
2949(?)	Mottled green ground, Chinaland pattern as above. **Chinaland**
2950	Royal blue lustre ground, chinese landscape, figures and pagoda all in underglaze colours. **Chinaland**
2971	Emerald green ground with black friezes. Main design is Chinoiserie pattern as 2481. Friezes contain cartouches with oriental scenes. **Temple**
2971(?)	Fish
2972	Deep blue ground, Chinoiserie pagodas and bridges with six figures.
2979(A)	Orange lustre ground with gilt interior, and frieze band of gilt tracery on black. (For coffee set)
2975	Matt peach lustre ground, tube – lined flowers and foliage in orange, green, blue and yellow.
3013	Orange lustre ground with wide white frieze decorated with brown 'crazing'. Matt black inside(?)
3015	Mottled red ground, mountains, trees, terraces and pagoda in natural underglaze colours. **Chinaland**
3016	Parrots.
3017	Matt black ground with coloured friezes, ground decorated with parrot in red, yellow, blue and green. **Parrots**
3023	Royal blue lustre ground with butterflies and spider's webs in delicate gilt with underglaze colouring. **New Flies**
3025	Blue lustre ground, butterflies and spider's webs in delicate gilt with rich underglaze colouring. **New Flies**
—	Orange lustre ground as 3023/5 above
—	Pink lustre ground as 3023/5 above
3026	As 2481 with white/cream ground. **Temple**
3026b	Vellum ground with bird of paradise with long plumed tail flying among oriental trees with fruit and foliage (See 3155) **Paradise Bird and Tree**
3027	As 2941 with cream ground and black friezes. **Temple**
3037	Orange lustre ground with Parrots in shades of green, blue and yellow perched on foliage. **Parrots**
3041	Dark blue lustre ground, with realistic apples and blossom.
3042	Dark blue lustre ground with embossed decoration of oranges and leaves. **Orange Embossed**
3046	Mottled blue ground with illustration of bird with a pine cone in colours and gilt. **Bird and Pine Cone**
3047	Ivory ground with pattern of pagodas and oriental motifs, frieze in terracotta.
3048	As 2941 with cream ground and blue friezes. **Temple**
3050	Royal blue ground, Persian style flowers and foliage. **Turkish**
3052	Dimpled pearl lustre ground with embossed decoration of oranges and leaves **Orange Embossed**
3053	Rust high glaze, with royal blue frieze overlaid with gilt tracery to show blue through in rounds. (For Coffee set).
3064	Orange ground with fruit clusters and blossom. **Orchard**
3071	Blue ground with stylised flowers, and border and frieze. **Turkish**
3073	Deep blue ground, pattern as 3074 below. **Paradise Bird and Tree**
3074	Red mottled ground with bird of paradise flying past stylised cloud and tree with foliage. N.B. Cloud not always present. **Paradise Bird and Tree**
3075	Matt mottled orange ground with bird of paradise flying past stylised cloud and foliage. **Paradise Bird and Tree**
3093	Temple Flowers
3130	Green ground with black grounded friezes. Printed and painted in colours and gilt, main pagoda with large circular opening, bridge and trees, two figures in a boat, friezes with cartouches containing oriental scenes. **Temple**
3141	Cream ground with stylised 'umbrella' shaped trees in blue and green. **Landscape Tree**
3142	Pearl ground with stylised, 'umbrella' shaped trees in orange and green. **Landscape Tree**
3143	Mottled black and red, bird of paradise flying across cloud, above exotic oriental tree with pendant foliage. **Paradise Bird and Tree** (*sometimes with Cloud*)
3144	Mottled light blue ground with long tailed bird of paradise flying past stylised cloud and tree with foliage. Underglaze colours and gilt. **Paradise Bird and Tree**
3145	Terracotta ground with characters of oriental writing, gilt fishes and other items in green and blue on black medallions, gilt and coloured frieze at base.
3147	Matt black ground with bird of paradise in red, green and brown underglaze enamels. **Paradise Bird and Tree**
3151	Mustard yellow ground with bird of paradise in red, green and brown underglaze enamels. **Paradise Bird and Tree**
3154	Mottled orange ground, bird of paradise flying past stylised foliage. **Paradise Bird and Tree**
3155	Dark blue ground with butterflies and bird of paradise flying past stylised oriental tree, colours and gilt (see also 3026b) **Paradise Bird and Tree**
3158	Matt black ground with white friezes containing cartouches with oriental scenes. Main pattern is **Mikado** (see 2881)

3159	Blue ground with Bird(s) of Paradise flying from left to right among butterflies and exotic trees with hanging foliage in colours of red, orange, yellow and blue. **Paradise Bird and Tree**
3178	Terracotta ground with matt black panel and underglaze enamels showing two chinese figures with pagodas. Broad frieze with plant leaves and round cartouches containing varied colourful pictures
3179	Rust coloured ground, oriental figures and pagoda on a black panel, Elaborate gilt and coloured frieze.
3188	Mottled red ground, stylised flowers and foliage.
3190	Red ground with cross shaped medallion of stylised flowers and berries, two butterflies n black and white. *Cubist Butterfly*
3193	Pale blue ground with sprays of prunus blossom
3194	Blue ground with outlined stems of bush topped by bold, stylised flowerheads, (with butterfly ?) *Cubist Butterfly*
3195	Orange lustre ground, with black, rugged stems extending in a cross from central medallion to stylised flowers and butterflies. *Cubist Butterfly*
3196	Dark blue ground, with bird of paradise and cloud motifs in colours and gilt. **Chinese Bird**
3197	Dark blue ground, exotic birds and curly flowers and foliage in near 'paisley pear' style in both under and overglaze colours and gilt. **Chinese Bird**
3199	Blue ground, figures before pagodas, enamelled and gilded, with frieze of oriental writing characters in gilt. *Chinese Figures*
3234	Handcraft. Cream ground with pattern of overlapping scales outlined in brown, each scale having a group of five coloured 'petals'.
3235	Handcraft. White ground with blue borders, and large three-lobed flowers in blue, outlined in orange. **Shamrock**
3236	Handcraft. Bluebells, three and four-lobed flowers on a blue ground in shades of rust, blue, green and lavender. *Floribunda*
3237	Deep blue ground with dominant dragon in colours/gilt. **Dragon and Cloud**
3239	Pale mottled ground with stylised slender tree rising to wide pendulous canopy of foliage, with bird flying past. **Tree and Swallow**
3241	Bird of Paradise in flight against a mottled red ground. **Paradise Bird and Tree**
3242	Handcraft. Matt glaze, blue yellow & lavender stylised cornflowers. Base of vases banded in stripes of navy and lavender, plaque with stripes as a cross from central medallion. **Flowering Papyrus**. See also 3648
3243	Matt blue ground, stylised Swallows flying before clouds. **Paradise Bird and Tree?**
3244	Matt glaze, blue ground, exotic trees with birch-like white/black trunks and pendant foliage in lavender orange and gilt. **Forest Tree**
3251	Blue ground with oriental gilded dragon. **Dragon and Cloud**
3253	Blue ground. **Forest Tree**
3255	Handcraft. Central floral medallion with star containing Irises, fan shapes and floral motifs in mauve blue green, yellow and black.
3265	Cream/mauve. **Forest Tree** (?). See also 3244
3270	**Diaper**
3271	Handcraft. Cream ground with mauve, blue and yellow flowers outlined in blue.
3272	Blue ground with pattern of crude stems and sprays of leaves behind yellow and red cherries. **Cherry**
3273	Handcraft. White ground with friezes of turquoise and aquamarine, spikes of simplified Delphiniums rising from lower frieze. **Delphinium**
3274	Matt blue ground with 'tiled' or 'scaled' finish, pattern as 3275 below. **Chinese Bird and Cloud**
3275	Matt orange/yellow ground, Bird of Paradise flying past stylised clouds, near gnarled tree with foliage in black, blue and green. Colourful underglaze enamels. **Chinese Bird and Cloud**
3278	Royal blue ground with stylised Honesty branches and 'discs' outlined in black, coloured in pale lemon and blue. **Honesty**
3279	Pale blue ground with birds flying past slender tree with wide canopy of pendulous foliage. **Tree and Swallow**
3280	Pale blue ground, pattern as 3239 above. **Tree and Swallow**
3281	Speckled cream ground with pair of birds flying past slender tree with purple and orange foliage and shrub below. **Tree and Swallow**
3283	Blue ground, pattern as 3244 above. **Forest Tree** (?)
3285	Matt blue ground with Swallows flying before stylised tree with pendant foliage. **Tree and Swallow**
3297	Handcraft. Pink ground, diagonal panels of flowers and chevrons, patterned borders. *Farrago*
3305	Handcraft. Pale matt ground with bold, simplified leaves, bubbles and butterfly. *Carnival*
3320	**New Chinese Bird and Cloud**
3321	Golden buff ground with oriental bird and flowers, bird turning his neck to look backwards at his feet (Angry Bird!) **New Chinese Bird and Cloud**
3322	Dark ground with highly ornamental bird of paradise in green, yellow, purple and blue flying before red stylised cloud, and turning his head to look back at his feet. **New Chinese Bird and Cloud**
3324	Fruit

3325	Handcraft. Rust ground with bold decoration in yellow-beige stripes and panels around very stylised tri-partite deco flower. *Orchid*
3326	*Stellata*
3331	Matt green ground, Chinese style dragon in gilt and colours. **Dragon and Cloud**
3332	Electric blue ground with Chinese style dragon in gilt and colours. **Dragon and Cloud**
3334	Orange lustre ground with sprays of stylised geometric foliage including sickle shaped leaves, and incorporating stylised sunflowers rising from base. *Geometric Sunflower*
3341	*Daisy and Stripe*
3350	Matt ground in mottled medium/light blue, with bird of paradise and stylised oriental tree in black, orange and gilt, with some top enamelling. **Paradise Bird and Tree**
3351	Red ground with oriental dragon among small stylised clouds. **Dragon and Cloud**
3352	Mottled dark red ground with lightning flashes and bubbles in blue, green, gold and black. **Jazz**
3353	Mottled orange ground with lightning flashes and bubbles in shades of green, blue, gold and black. **Jazz**
3354	Matt blue mottled glaze, Bird of paradise on stylised blossom bough. *Feathertailed Bird and Flower*
3355	Green ground, pattern as 3354 above. *Feathertailed Bird and Flower*
3356	Lightning motif in light and dark blue, bronze copper lustre and gilt – for coffee set. **Zig Zag**
3357	Matt tan brown ground, with black pattern with silver zig-zags rising from base towards top edged in orange, brown and silver.**Zig Zag**
3358	Handcraft. Grey-green ground nearly covered by large blue flowers with yellow centres with black, worm-like stamens.
3360	**Fish and Seaweed** (See also 2440)
3361	Dark blue ground, pattern as 3352 above. **Jazz**
3385	Matt pale green ground with pattern as 3387 below. *Floral Comets*
3387	Matt green ground with three posies of stylised flowerheads each at the end of a triple banded 'comet's tail' or multiple coloured 'medal ribbon'. *Floral Comets*
3388	Matt pale blue ground, stylised, long-tailed swallows flying among exotic bushes and trees in cypress shapes. **Fantasia**
3389	Matt lilac ground, pattern as 3388 above. **Fantasia**
3394	Pale ground with naturalistic bird with plumed tail, sitting on branch with foliage. **Bird on a Bough**
3396	Sharp green lustre ground with spires of daisy-like flowers painted in many colours. **Garden**
3400	**Fantasia** (see 3421)
3401	Pale blue ground with stylised posies of flowers and leaves at the end of bold, curving, cross-banded 'ribands'. *Floral Comets*. (See also 3405 and 3387)
3405	Pale blue ground with stylised posies of flowers and leaves at the end of 'ribands'. See 3387 *Floral Comets*
3406	Dark blue ground, green long-tailed swallows above exotic plants. see also 3421 **Fantasia**
3412	Matt blue ground with lifelike Kingfisher in flight.
3413	Handcraft. Mottled blue ground with stylised flowers and foliage in shades of blue, yellow, mauve, red and orange. **Garden**
3417	Yellow ground with black edging, with pattern of pale green and lilac leaves, blue twigs and spray of red cherries. **Cherry**
3419	Handcraft, blue ground, almost obscured by bold, bulbous, cloud-like shapes in red, green and yellow, all outlined in gilt *Aurora* (?)
3420	Stylised city skyline in blue against dramatic banded sky in shades of yellow and mauve. *Metropolis*
3421	Powder blue ground with long-tailed birds hovering above exotic plants in 'cypress tree' shapes, and flowers all in reds, blues and gilt. **Fantasia**
3424	Pinky beige ground, with stylised, umbrella shaped tree, and flower of abstract design, slightly resembling a pansy, with stiff, spikey leaves. *Prickly Pansy*
3428	Dark blue ground with stylised posies of flowers and leaves at the end of bold, curving, cross-banded 'ribands'. *Floral Comets*. (See also 3405 and 3387)
3438	Handcraft. Stylised foliage in mauve, blue, yellow and black, with navy horizontal lines.
3439	Red and black mottled ground, with stylised, angular flowers some almost naive in angular simplicity, colours are underglaze
3440	Camouflage
3446	Handcraft. Matt pink ground with large flowerheads in yellow, red and blue.
3447	Pale blue ground with single dramatic flower with jagged outline and corona growing from low, jagged foliage. *Explosion*
3448	Pale blue ground with large orange/tan flowerheads, with turquoise and orange centres. *Peach Melba*
3449	Mottled red ground with geometric band of foliage & flowers. *Prickly Pansy*
3450	Matt mottled light brown ground with pale brown clouds with jagged blue centres, stylised and ornate 'sun' in colours and gilt rising from behind colourful, ornamented hills. *Awakening*
3451	Handcraft. Crinoline lady with parasol strolling on garden terrace, with rose bush to left of figure. Shades of blue, orange, yellow and cream. **Victorian Lady**
3452	Dark blue ground, butterflies & star-shaped floral clusters
3453	Matt blue ground, otherwise as 3450. *Awakening*

3454	*Explosion*, See 3447 above.
3456	Mottled rouge ground, otherwise as 3450. *Awakening*
3457	Mottled ground with group of overlapping stylised flowerheads and projecting jagged foliage. *Jagged Bouquet*
3458	Beige ground, with Disney-like tall castle in black or dark brown silhouette in background, rocks and trees in the foreground. **Witch's Castle**
3465	Mauve and lilac mottled ground, 'banded' construction with primula-like flowers in pink and yellow.
3471	Brown background with spires of multi-coloured daisy-like flowers. **Garden**
3476	Mottled yellow and green ground with stylised tree casting a shadow.
3478	Mottled orange ground with spires of colourful daisy-like flowers. **Garden**
3489	*Jagged Bouquet*, See 3457
3491	Picture of 'Victorian' female figure wearing a crinoline skirt, standing in a garden terrace with spires of coloured flowers. **Victorian Lady**
3496	Pale green ground, otherwise as 3450. *Awakening*
3497	*Awakening* as 3450 but with different ground
3498	Handcraft. Mottled blue and white ground with stylised Irises in pink and blue growing from short foliage. **Iris**
3500	Cream ground with simple pattern of slim 'deco' type trees of poplar shape in solid red, black and blue. **Sylvan Glade**
3501	Mottled brown ground with spires of coloured, stylised flowers. **Garden**
?3501	Pale blue ground shading to white, with gilt reeds and grasses below wild ducks both in colours and in shadow only flying left to right. **Wild Duck**
3503	Handcraft. Streaked yellow ground, with pendant sprays of flowers and foliage in shades of blue and pink. *Jazz Poppies*
3504	*Rose Marie*
3505	Matt orange ground with black and white stemmed trees by a lily pond in purple, blue, orange, black, white and gilt. *Geometric Tree*
3506	Dark blue ground with enamels outlining a lady dancing in 'gypsy' style with swirling skirts.
3507	Matt green ground with design of grasses, ornamental poppy flowers and leaves. *Iceland Poppy*
3508	Handcraft. Cream ground with 'brush-marks' in yellow, pink and blue, with flowers in red/yellow and two-tone blue surrounded by green and blue borders. *Wind & Flower*
3509	Leaf green ground with completely underglaze pattern comprising a sinuous tree with foliage in dark blue and green.
3517	Tableware pattern of stylised trees in orange, green, yellow and black on a pale yellow ground, with fern fronds at base. **Autumn Trees and Fern**
3519	Pale ground with entirely handpainted pattern comprising a multi-coloured diagonal swirl, with large bold stylised flowerheads below and half showing above. **Freehand Red Sunflower**
3522	Handcraft. Ice blue ground with black and grey boughs and pink flowers. **Apple Blossom**
3523	Handcraft. Matt pale blue ground with bold, simple trees with yellow, brown and red foliage. *Parkland*
3524	Matt green ground with pale green tree trunk and branches over dense foliage in autumn colours. *Parkland*
3525(?)	Mottled yellow ground with large Bird of Paradise of many colours with wings spread, and head turned up among exotic flowers. **Chinese Bird**
3525	Handcraft. Large Clematis flowers in blue and magenta with black and green leaves almost covering mottled beige ground. **Clematis**
3526	Handcraft. Dark blue ground with spires of delphiniums and other stylised flowers in blue, pink, green and black. **New Delphinium**
3529	Black high glaze ground with exotic oriental bird perched on a waterlily. *Crested Bird and Waterlily*
3530	Mottled red ground with exotic oriental crested bird perched on a waterlily. *Crested Bird and Waterlily*
3535	
3536	Mottled red ground with ornamental flowers and bird. *Crested Bird and Waterlily*
3544	Mottled orange ground, birds of paradise and stylised flowerheads.
3546	Ivory and pale blue coffee set, pattern as 3547 below. *Diamond*
3547	Green ground with black lower (or central) portion, gilded round edge, and to divide portions. Gilded Diamond at divide. Coffee set. *Diamond*
3551	Black ground, mostly obscured by design of red circular medallion (if plate) with fringes of yellow and then purple. If cup, red is lower portion. *Eclipse*
3552	Russet red ground with pink lower band (cup), decorated with a deco fan pattern inclined to one side with panels in black, yellow, green, blue and mauve, the whole outlined in gilt, white and blue. Matt black interior. *Deco Fan*
3553	Matt black ground, with diagonal, wavy stripes in gilt, beige, green and white. *Strata*
3554	Matt black ground, with pattern of vertical columns of varying lengths descending from the top rim in group, with gilt columns alternating with blue, green, yellow, cream and orange. Coffee set.
3557	Deep blue ground, exotic circular flowerheads in front of a fan of coloured panels, yellow, green, orange and blue, with gilding. **Fan**

3558	Mottled red ground, exotic circular flowerheads in front of a fan of coloured panels, yellow, green, orange and blue, with clouds of dots and gilding. **Fan**
3562	Black and aquamarine ground with stylised flowers in red, yellow and blue, bird in song. **Nightingale**
3563	Handcraft. Blue ground with stylised black and white slender trees with green foliage in front of a cottage with a red roof – all rather in the style of Clarice Cliff.
3564	Royal blue lustre ground with motif of fairy, and vertically curving bands of brightly coloured flowers against a curving line. Designs are in gilt with underglaze enamels. **Fairy**
3566	Dark blue ground with top enamelled right-angle shapes and tile-like squares in yellow and red overlapping. 'Modern Art' style. Top rim has semi-circular florets. *Geometrica*
3567	Ground shaded in bands from palest blue to mid purply-blue, with stylised sun shown in concentric bands from purple centre centre to yellow then orange outer, shining on large stylised blue and purple flowerheads and leaves. Border is banded in beige, brown and orange, and has continuous geometric pattern like large purple saw teeth. **Russian**
3569	Green high glaze ground with pattern showing a tree in black/navy silhouette.
3570	Matt turquoise glaze with rectangles and chevrons in black, red, yellow, mauve and green. Bauhaus in style. *Mondrian*
3571	*Apples and Grapes*
3576	Deep orange lustre ground with diagonal panels of flowers in blue, yellow and purple, edged on one side by gilt wavy line. Picture of a hovering winged fairy, with enlarged black silhouette. Colours are all underglaze. **Fairy**
3587	*Medley* (See 3593)
3588	Slightly ribbed appearance, finished in parallel bands of green, blue, turquoise and orange with upper section finished as simplistic flowers in green and orange. *Medley*
3589	Bold, stylised flowerheads formed of concentric circles in yellow and orange, outlined in blue, with single feathers projecting from behind. *Hiawatha*
3593	Slightly ribbed appearance, finished in parallel bands in various shades of green, blue, turquoise and orange. *Medley*
3594	Red ground, with dragon confronting traveller, coloured in sepia, black and gilt. **Chinese Dragon**
3595	Turquoise ground, with dragon confronting a traveller, coloured in sepia black and gilt. **Chinese Dragon**
3597	As 3594 above, but with blue ground. **Chinese Dragon**
3598	Dark blue lustre ground with underglaze enamels portraying a Nightingale in full song, sitting on a bush. **Nightingale**
3599	*Medley* (See 3593)
3600	*Medley* (See 3593)
3601	Blue ground with complex single flowerheads in enamels, mainly pink mauve, orange and yellow, above underglaze single leaves.
3601A	Mottled pink ground with blue flowers, otherwise similar to 3601 above
3606	Green (or other) ground overlaid in bright yellows with flowers and butterflies. *Dahlia and Butterfly*
3615	Blue ground with stylised circular flowerheads and angular panels in brown, orange black, fawn and gilt. *Scimitar*
3645	Mottled red ground with ladies before pagodas and bridges, highlighted in gilt.
3646	Pattern as 3507 above. *Iceland Poppy*
3648	Handcraft. White ground with sprays of stylised cornflowers and vertical stripes in shades of blue, yellow and lavender. See also 3242 **Flowering Papyrus**
3650	Handcraft, handpainted pattern in blue, then green brushstrokes radiating out from the centre. Similar to 3773
3651	Ground of blue, green and purple teardrops with stylised circular flowerheads and angular panels in black, yellow, orange, fawn and gilt. *Scimitar*
3653	See 3654 below. *Mandarins Chatting*
3654	Black ground with vibrant green friezes and two Chinese figures in bright enamels in conversation beneath a stylised tree. *Mandarins Chatting*
3655	Geometric pattern in orange, brown, yellow and black in chevrons, circles and grids in graph-like formation. **Jazz Stitch**
3656	See 3660 below. **Chinese Dragon**
3657	Geometric design, shades of black and green with gilt. *Chevrons*
3658	Abstract pattern of solid squares and rectangles in black with silver outlining, on a pale green ground. **Carre**
3659	See 3658 above. **Carre**
3660	Yellow ground with chinese figure confronting a dragon in gilt, green and black. **Chinese Dragon**
3663	Handcraft. Black reserve with vivid multi-coloured flowers some with spiky outlines with stems and leaves. *Summer Medley*
3667	Handcraft. White central ground with pattern of big, bold stylised flowers similar to harebells or tulips in colours of pink, yellow and red. Frieze is blue with yellow, toothed pattern like the rays of the sun. **Tiger Lily**

3675	Cream ground with dark red friezes, and two oriental figures under frieze of flowers and foliage in colours & gilt. *Mandarins Chatting*
3678	*Diamond*
3681	Dark blue ground with handles (to coffee cups, or lids) formed as arched near nude female figures. *Bathing Belle*
3684	White, Gold and Black, with 'Bathing Belle' figures. For Coffee Set. *Bathing Belle*
3690	Cream ground with gold lined black border and pattern in bold stripes in red, black and gold intersecting at angles. (for coffee set) *Intersections*
3691	Shaded light green ground with aster-like flowers in yellow, pink and orange, with dark green leaves. **Daisy**
3692	Tangerine ground slashed with black white and gilt lightning flashes. *Lightning*
3693	Handcraft. Dark blue reserve with daisy like flowers in shades of yellow, orange, pink and white, with stems and light green leaves. **Daisy**
3694	Handcraft. Mottled orange reserve with multi-coloured spiky-edged flowers in mauve, yellows and pinks, with leaves in shades of yellow, green and bottle green. **Anemone**
3695	Mottled red ground, with elaborate geometric flowerhead in fan shape, resembling Egyptian papyrus, also tapering spears of multi-coloured flowers. **Egyptian Fan**
3696	Dark blue ground with elaborate geometric flowerhead in fan shape resembling Egyptian papyrus, also tapering spears of multi-coloured flowers. **Egyptian Fan**
3697	Pale blue ground with elaborate geometric flowerhead in fan shape, resembling Egyptian papyrus, also tapering spears of multicoloured flowers. **Egyptian Fan**
3698	Pale blue ground with elaborate geometric flowerhead in fan shape, resembling Egyptian papyrus, also tapering spires of multicoloured flowers. **Egyptian Fan**
3699	Orange ground, exotic flowers held by fan shaped motifs and curved lines. *Rainbow Fan*
3700	Mottled turquoise ground with sweeping curved lines and fan shapes in shades of pale blue, black, primrose and rust. *Rainbow Fan*
3701	Black ground with red friezes, and leaves in gilt, red and yellow.
3702	See 3703 below. *Mandarin Tree*
3703	Cream ground with mottled red borders overlaid with coloured flowerheads in enamels and gilt. Main body has piles of rocks from which grow stunted oriental trees, and shrubs with black spiky leaves and flowerheads in pink, orange and blue *Mandarin Tree*
3713	Blue ground, pattern as 3700. *Rainbow Fan*
3714	(Handcraft) Matt green ground with design of flowers. **Daisy**
3716	*Lightning* (See also 3692)
3718	Handcraft. Ground yellow at the top, shaded through to brown, the whole showing a pattern of vertica 'brushstrokes'.
3719	Cream ground with mottled green borders overlaid with coloured flowerheads in enamels and gilt. Main body has piles of rocks from which grow stunted oriental trees, and shrubs with black spiky leaves and flowerheads in pink, orange and blue. *Mandarin Tree*
3721	Pale blue ground, pattern as 3700. *Rainbow Fan*
3745	Handcraft. Mottled pale pink and blue ground, with simplistic blue, pink and yellow flowers. **Primula**
3746	Beige ground. **Primula**
3750	Matt ground in vivid purple shading to turquoise blue, with abstract patterns in straight lines, chevrons and panels in black also rectangular panels in red, purple and green. *Mondrian*
3765	Turquoise ground, otherwise as 3769. *Mephistopheles*
3765a	Turquoise ground with exotic flowers in colours and gilt beneath a tree laden with eye motifs as blossoms *Devil's Copse*
3766	Matt, warm beige ground, with handpainted, naturalistic twig bearing leaves in autumn colours. **Autum Leaf**
3767	Pale blue ground, Mephistopheles figure dressed in bright red in a tropical landscape with exotic flower and bushes, and a black and white banded tree with eye-like blossom among pendulous foliage, and swag of berries in orange, red, green and white. *Mephistopheles*
3769	Yellow ground, Mephistopheles figure dressed in bright red in a tropical landscape with exotic flowers and bushes, and a black and white banded tree with eye-like blossom among pendulous foliage, and swags o berries in orange, red, green and white. *Mephistopheles*
3771	Ribbed appearance, with matt slip glazes in varied colours. A 'Stoneware' pattern.
3773	Handpainted yellow background with jagged, painted pattern in green and blue radiating out from centre
3774	Cream ground with multi-coloured stylised flowers held by curving lines. *Bell*
3785	Matt pale blue ground with harebells and flowerheads in colours and gilt. *Bell*
3786	Mottled green ground with triangular panels of lilac and pale blue made up of many flowerheads, an between these panels large, single, stylised flowerheads of many colours, each trailing a kite-like tail c bluebells. *Bell*
3787	Blue ground, mottled exotic tree with pendant foliage, and blossoms like eye motifs, bushes and plant below with bold paddle and arrow shaped leaves, enamelled in many bright colours. *Devil's Copse*

3788	Mottled red ground, with triangular panels of blue and pale green made up of many flowerheads, and between these panels large, single stylised flowerheads of many colours, each trailing a kite-like tail of bluebells. *Bell*
3789	Powder blue ground, otherwise as 3790. **Gum Flower**
3790	Mottled green and yellow ground, decorated with sprays of trumpet shaped pink flowers and seed pods. **Gum Flower**
3794	Matt sage green ground with highly stylised flowers and leaves.
3796	Mid blue ground with green handles and borders – handles as arched female figures in gilt bathing costume. *Bathing Belle*
3801	Black ground (with grey border to lid), enamelled flowers including foxglove, poppy and delphinium in yellow, blue and orange.
3802	Yellow ground decorated with brown brush strokes and large, Daisy-like flower with petals of various colours, other flowers and foliage. **Autumn Daisy**
3803	Pale green ground with paintbrush strokes in mauve. Black borders, with linked, curved sections in pink, blue, yellow and orange, and spray of slender, pointed, multi-coloured flowers radiating from centre.
3803(?)	'Liberty' style bands rising from base in colours of black, white, gold, mauve, green, orange and yellow. Above these a white ground covered with paint daubs in pale green and grey, with partial flowers painted in. Upper frieze is a series of black rectangles alternating above and below a horizontal line.
3804	Possibly a 'Stoneware' pattern
3813	Mottled pink ground with slender deco black stems topped by exotic circular flowerheads with radial panels, heavily decorated in colours and gilt. **Wagon Wheels**
3814	Mottled red ground with stylised circular flowerheads with radial petals and foliage in colours and gilt. **Wagon Wheels**
3815	Powder blue ground, with pattern of two large flowers in orange, mauve and gilt. Border features a series of stepped, angled panels imitating embroidery in gilt, with crescents and chevrons in orange, green and yellow enamels. *Needlepoint*
3816	Mottled red ground with flowers in colours and gilt. **Wagon Wheels**
3817	Mottled pale turquoise ground, with very stylised, multi-coloured flowers and leaves beneath pendant tree foliage with eye-like fruit. Colours and gilt, *Devil's Copse*
3818	Mottled greeny yellow ground with Hollyhocks in shades of pink and red, with circular pale green leaves. **Hollyhocks**
3819	Mottled blue ground with stylised hollyhock flowers rising in a spike, with foliage in colours and gilt. **Hollyhocks**
3820	As 3819, with black ground. **Hollyhocks**
3827	Green ground with foxgloves and other flowers growing up in spires, enamels and gilt
3829	Possibly a 'Stoneware' Pattern
3837	Handcraft. Cream ground with pink edges, brown herbiage with spikes of blue, pink and brown flowers.
3842	Possibly Stoneware, uniform, plain, muddy green colour.
3843	Plain sharp green ground with gilt border and handles – for deco style dish, shape no. 1341-2
3845	Ribbed appearance, painted in horizontal bands of pink, green, blue and brown. *Medley*
3846	Plain black lustre ground, with wide band of gilding to borders.
3848	Pale green ground with sprays of flowers in yellow, orange, green, purple and blue.
3849	Black ground with perimeter decorated with pattern of flowers in colours and gilt.
3857	Blue ground with a pattern of fronds of trailing leaves in green and gilt, with pendant, orange drop-shaped berries. **Leaf**
3858	Black, high glaze ground with pattern of simple stylised flowers in rather '1960s' style, in underglaze white and gilt
3860	Dark red ground, Chinoiserie pattern, (see 2728). **New Mikado**
3863	Pale green ground with stylised deco tree, bushes and flowers in foreground, path leading to garden gate in background with bushes. **Garden Gate**
3865	Handcraft. Grey ground with blue round base, and pattern showing a tree with flowers in many colours.
3866	Pinky purple ground with festoons of pendant blue flowers. **Wisteria**
3867	Turquoise green ground, shading darker at edges, with sprays of yellow flowers. **New Laburnham**
3868	Pale matt green ground, with simplistic primula-like flowers in yellow and orange with stylised leaves behind. **Vogue**
3873	**Leaf** (see 3857)
3874	Mottled grey ground with naturalistic Bluebells and Primulas growing among foliage and grasses round a pond or cave. *Bluebells* (but see 4120)
3875	Naturalistic Bluebells and Primulas growing among foliage and grasses round a cave or pond. *Bluebells* (See 4120)
3886a	Two tone turquoise green ground for Moderne coffee set.
3887a	Matt grey ground with blue bases and handles – for Moderne 'Tea for Two'.
3888a	Two tone blue ground for Moderne coffee set.

3889	Mottled red and black ground, with flame shaped flowers, and ragged foliage hanging from above, exotic bird in colours and gilt flying from right to left. **Sketching Bird**
3890	Pale mauve ground, flame shaped, pastel coloured plants below, ragged foliage hanging from above, with exotic bird flying past.**Sketching Bird**
3891	Cream ground shading down to grey, exotic tree with pendant foliage, exotic bird flying past. **Sketching Bird**
3892	Dark blue high glazed ground with sprays of delicate, exotic flowers and foliage in top enamelled colours and gilt (see 3894). **Persian Garden**
3893	Black high glaze ground, pattern as 3892. **Persian Garden**
3894	Matt pale turquoise ground shading at borders to navy, with sprays of exotic flowers and foliage in colours and gilt. **Persian Garden**
3896(?)	Pale grey ground with eggshell finish glaze, and motif of a slender, black deco tree bearing varied enamelled flowers in orange, blues, pink, mauve and brown
3897	Pale peach ground with eggshell finish glaze, and motif of a slender, black deco tree with varied enamelled flowers on it in orange, blues, pink, mauve and brown.
3901	Beige ground, shading to blue at extremes, with pattern of simplistic flowers in orange and yellow with green leaves. Enamels of the pattern are thick, raising the pattern above the dark outlines. **Incised Diamond**
3907	Pale blue lustre ground, exotic bird in flight. **Sketching Bird**
3912	Beige ground with large blue/green spots. 'Spots'
3913	Handcraft. Pale beige ground with abstract flower in blue, yellow and brown. *Floral Mist*
3917	Pattern like paint running in shades of lemon, pale blue and turquoise on cream.
3919	Pale ground, design of natural leaf and catkin. Used for jug *Leaf and Catkin*
3922	Red ground with wild grasses and shrubs below, ducks in detail and in shadow shape only flying left to right, colours and gilt. **Wild Duck**
3923	Yellow ground, otherwise as 3922 above. **Wild Duck**
3924	Blue ground, otherwise as 3922 above. **Wild Duck**
3926	Pale yellow high glaze ground with green lustre borders, with sharply depicted poppies and meadow flowers in bright colours and gilt. *Summer Flowers*
3927	Cream ground, with groups of richly enamelled, stylised flowers in orange, mauve, yellow, black and blue. *Summer Flowers*
3939	Cream ground with hand applied slip to give loose bands of green, brown, mauve and blue.
3943(?)	Pale blue ground, with pattern of realistic leaves, and florets of Hydrangea in gilt and coloured enamels. *Lace Cap Hydrangea*
3943	**Tubelined Tree**
3944	Handcraft Matt blue-green ground with gum tree design
3945	(Handcraft) Matt cream ground with design of voluminous leaves, plus one flower like a blue and turquoise tree with stamens, one like a yellow papyrus blossom – all tubelined **Tubelined Flower**
3946	Handcraft. Matt cream ground with design of hazel nuts and leaves in a mixture of very soft pinks and blues
3948	As 3950 below, but with pale turquoise ground. **Flower and Falling Leaf**
3949	As 3950 below, but with dark red lustre ground.**Flower and Falling Leaf**
3950	Shaded cream ground with exotic, complex, geometric flowerheads, some 'full-face', some 'in profile' in colours and gilt, also trimming of a few natural leaves. **Sketching Bird**
3952	Blue ground with ornamental bird flying past sinuous tree with branches full of fan-shaped, coloured blossom. **Flower and Falling Leaf**
3957	Cream ground with illustration of galleon at sea, painted in shades of blue and pink.
3965 (?)	Turquoise ground with scarlet figure of Mephistopheles standing near tree with black and white spiral trunk and coloured fruits like eyes. In foreground are exotic plants with paddle shaped blossoms and arrow like leaves, all painted with many brightly coloured enamels. *Mephistopheles*
3965	Deep red ground with ornamental heron flying past sinuous tree with branches full of fan-shaped, coloured blossom. *Heron and Magical Tree*, see 4160
—	Also found with acid green ground. *Heron and Magical Tree*
3966	Pale green ground, tree in shades of green with Hydrangea leaves and blossom in colours and gilt. *Lace Cap Hydrangea*
3967	Dark red ground, with coloured Hydrangea florets backed by life-like leaves. *Lace Cap Hydrangea*
—	Pink ground, Hydrangea pattern as 3967 (see above)
3968	Blue ground with white flowers like small wild Roses, green leaves.
3971	Primrose ground shading to blue upper and lower borders, with ornamental fish bearing large flowing fins coloured in top enamels in green, yellow, mauve and orange among flowing seabed plants. **River Fish (Shabunkin)**
3972	Orange lustre ground with spires of Hollyhock plants bearing blue, pink, mauve, yellow and green flowers **Hollyhocks**
3973	Green ground with stylised flowers and foliage in colours. **Hollyhocks**
3974	Exotic, highly decorated fish in delicate, flowing seabed scene. **River Fish (Shabunkin)** (See 3971)

3975	Warm beige ground with matt glaze, and pattern of stylised bluebells and large flowerhead in orange, cream, blue and green, the whole tubelined in the Charlotte Rhead style. Copies Charlotte Rhead's *Persian Rose*
3976	Pale beige ground, with numerous bands of straight and wavy lines in colours of pink and mauve.
3986	Cream ground with stylised flowers and foliage in colours and gilt.
3989	Blue ground, mottled exotic tree with pendant foliage, and blossoms like eye motifs, bushes and plants below. *Devil's Copse*
3990	Lemon ground, with seedheads and stylised flowers in colours and gilt.
3993	Yellow Buttercup (for floral embossed range)
3994	Pink Buttercup (for floral embossed range)
3997	Dark ground with brown tree trunk and branches almost obscured by hanging willow-like leaves in shades of pale and medium blue. *Forest Night*
4009	Plain lustred Rouge Royale with gilt edging
4012	Mottled cream ground with dark leaves and bold single coloured flowers in Lautrec poster style, with raised tubular edging. Flowers in shades of red and orange. **Tubelined Marigold**
4015	**Harebells**
4016	Pale ground with wide open Harebells growing on stems. **Harebells**
4017	Orange ground, otherwise as 4018. *Secretary Bird*
4018	Red ground with highly decorated tree and exotic bird with long legs and outstretched wings standing nearby. Design combines under and overglaze enamels and gilt. *Secretary Bird*
4019	Grey/green ground with naturalistic Squirrel. **Squirrel**
4060	For coffee set, pink glazed ground highlighted with gilt and black bands.
4076	For 'Tea for Two' set in Moderne design, lime green interior with rings in gilt, red, green, yellow, mauve, blue and white. *Tyrolean Bands*
4079	Green ground, with black and gilt banding, for coffee set
4083	Cream ground with Art Deco design in russet and brown stripe for coffee set.
4084	As 4083 above
4092	*Heatwave*
4103	Pale green ground, with gilt cobweb, fruiting branch above, harebells below, dragonfly in flight. **Spider's Web**
4108(?)	Pale green ground with bird flying past a willow tree in gilt and colours. **Sketching Bird**
4108	Pale green ground, with chinoiserie pattern. (see 2728). **New Mikado**
4118	Pale blue ground with gilt tree, and Bird of Paradise in front.
4120	Pale yellow ground with pendant leaves and stylised Primulas in pink and yellow underglaze colours round a pond or cave. **Primula and Leaf**
4123	Vivid green lustre ground, with grasses and seedheads
4125(?)	Pale blue ground with pendant leaves and stylised Primulas in pink and yellow underglaze colours round a pond or cave. **Primula and Leaf**
4125	Shaded green ground, varying to yellowish green, with pendant branches of willow bearing almost silhouetted brown leaves and white enamelled star-flowers, also one large flowerhead with star-like points, painted as dots in orange, lilac and green Bluebells grow up from the ground. *Babylon*
4126	*Babylon* (see 4125 above)
4136	Pale green ground with transfers of simple flowers in blue and brown. **Harebells**
4137	Graduated orange/brown ground with single large star-shaped flower in colours and gilt, with festoons of foliage and flowers hanging down each side, blue bell-like flowers on left, yellow and white blossoms on right. *Babylon*
4138	Semi-matt ground in shaded beige/brown, with stylised, curving and 'bulbous' representation of fields, trees and hills. Also seen as high glaze version in bright colours. **Tubelined Tree and Fields**
4140	Pale green ground with stylised Azalea flowers in pink growing on a twig, with leaves in green and yellow. **Azalea**
4146	**Spangled Tree**
4153	Pale yellow ground. *Heron and Magical Tree*
4154	Orange lustre ground with transfers of simple flowers in pink and blue. **Harebells**
4159	Dark red lustre ground, with heron flying past sinuous tree with branches bearing small, coloured fan-shaped flowers on them. Background foliage of tree hanging in shadow is in turquoise under glaze, heron and flowers are gilt & overglaze enamels. *Heron and Magical Tree*
4160	Green ground below, vivid blue above, with exotic bird flying past a twisted exotic tree with fans of blossom, gilded,, and black shadows. *Heron and Magical Tree*
4162	Green ground with stylised tulips and leaves in colours, and outlined with raised edges. **Tubelined Tulips**
4163	Shaded yellow ground, broad brown tree trunk with pendant green foliage and red blossoms to front, rearward foliage in deep, black shade. **Spangled Tree**
4178	Grey ground with gilt highlighting, for coffee set
4185	Pale green ground with slender tree having orange flowers. *Pastoral*
4186	Light blue ground with cockerells displaying near a bouquet of flowers, colours and gilt. *Fighting Cocks*

4190	Pale green ground, with pink flowers and yellow and green foliage
4194	Pale lemon ground. design of grasses and ornamental poppy flowers and leaves. *Iceland Poppy*
4208	Dark red ground with Chinoiserie design in colours and gilt as 2481. **Temple**
4212	*Fighting Cocks*
4215	Red ground with highly stylised 'deco' flowers, some as star-like flowerheads, some as lobed arcs or segments. *Starflower*
4217	Dark red lustre ground, with stylised tree with large, gnarled trunk and profuse pendant foliage – design in gilt alone. (See also 4241) **Tree and Clouds**
4218	Coral pink ground with dots, and posies of leaves in maroon, white and gilt scattered at intervals. *?Leaf and Dot*
4219	Very pale green ground, sprays of realistically depicted Anemones, with foliage in colours. **New Anemone**
4221	Pale ground with design of grasses and ornamental poppy flowers and leaves. *Iceland Poppy*
4225	Deep red ground with gilt rim and white enamel polka dots
4228	Pale green ground, with poppies in colours and gilt
4241	Deep red ground, with foliage rising from base with unusual striated colours, main feature is a bold tree with pendant green foliage and a black trunk patterned with bright green lobes and swirls. Top enamel flowers in red, lilac and yellow decorate the tree's foliage, and a butterfly is nearby. **Tree and Clouds**
4242	Pale blue pearly lustre ground with the **Spider's Web** pattern.
4243	Blue/grey ground, embossed flowers and spider's web. **Spider's Web**
4244	Powder blue lustre ground with decoration in colours and gilt showing bluebells and grasses overhung by bramble leaves with spider in a web. **Spider's Web**
4245	Mottled pink ground shading to blue, with pink and blue flowers. **New Anemone**
4246	Handcraft. Matt white ground with blue flowers with yellow centres, the whole surrounded by a yellow and blue frieze
4247	Orange ground with black silhouetted trees and grass,with light green foliage, rabbits shown in silhouette. **Rabbits at Dusk** (*Shadow Bunny*)
4249(?)	Lustre blue ground with butterflies flying among flower-laden pendant branches in colours.
4270	**Peggy**
4277	Yellow ground with slender, serrated green foliage hanging down, and yellow, multi-lobed flowers with orange stamens, the whole with black shading behind
4278	*Palm Blossom*
4282	Beige ground with natural, slightly spiky edged leaves in black, green and brown with Beech nuts opening to reveal the kernels. *Beech Nut*
4283	Pink ground with two storks wading under trees. Enamels and gilt. **New Stork**
4284	Black ground, otherwise as 3965. *Heron and Magical Tree*
4297	*Anthemis*
4298	Red ground with large, stylised flowers blooming at the top of a single curving stem like the trunk of a palm tree. *Palm Blossom*
4313	*Heron and Magical Tree*
4328(?)	Cream ground with chinoiserie pattern, (see 2728). **New Mikado**
4340	Rouge Royale. Deep red ground, Exotic wading birds grazing in water under trees, colours and gilt. **New Stork**
—	Green lustre ground with two exotic wading birds grazing in water under trees, colours and gilt. **New Stork**
—	Black ground, pattern as 4340 above. **New Stork**
—	Rouge Royale. Deep red ground, with bluebells and other flowers growing among grasses below, dragonflies and butterflies in flight, and a spider in a cobweb suspended from foliage with flowers above, colours and gilt. **Spider's Web**
—	Pink ground, pattern as above. **Spider's Web**
4347	Black ground, pattern as Rouge Royale version above
4385	Rouge Royale ground with pattern of vine and leaves in gilt, and grapes in colours and gilt. *Vine and Grape*
4433	Rouge Royale ground, with chinoiserie pattern. (see 2364). **Mikado**
4434	Blue lustre ground, with chinoiserie pattern, (see 2364). **Mikado**
4455	**Duck**
4488	Black (Noire Royale) ground with realistic flowers and leaves of Lily of the Valley. **Lily of the Valley**
4490	Black ground with realistic Mallard type ducks flying off to left above irises and wild grasses. **Duck**
4499	Red ground, otherwise as 4490 above. **Duck**
4519	Black ground with oriental couple under trees, colours and gilt.
4693	White glazed ground with groups of small coloured flowers. *Sunshine*
4753(?)	Blue ground with groups of yellow flowers and green and yellow butterflies. Coffee set has metal rims and handles
4754	Pale ground, with garden flowers and bluebirds. **Springtime**
4795	Mottled blue ground with twig of buds and blossom, bird of paradise and butterflies at periphery.
4809	Powder blue ground with thistleheads in enamels and gilt
4906	Primrose shading to cream ground, with floral decoration in colours and gilt.

4909	Blue background with litho medallion featuring bird with basket of fruit on a white ground.
4927	White ground with design of individual Chess pieces on a section of black and white chessboard.
5705	Handcraft. Pale blue ground with lightning like Zig-Zags in gilt and dark blue
5719	Yellow ground with broad frieze of various flowerheads and foliage on green background, main ground decorated with stylised flowering shrubs before stylised tree showing whole of trunk and branches in front of gilded foliage canopy.
5859	Mottled pink ground, shades of green and black forming silhouette scene of rabbits playing under tree. **Rabbits at Dusk** See also 4247
—	As 2728 above, but with Vert Royale ground. **New Mikado** (late version)
—	As 2728 above, but with pale green ground. **New Mikado** (late version)
—	As 2728 above, but with Bleu Royale ground. **New Mikado** (late version)
—	As 2728 above, but with Rouge Royale ground. **New Mikado** (late version)
—	As 2728 above, but with cream ground. **New Mikado** (late version)
—	As 2728 above, but with dark blue ground. **New Mikado** (late version)
—	Rouge Royale ground with design in both underglaze and overglaze colours depicting a turbanned Sultan regarding a small dark coloured picaninny, often with a palace in the background. *Sultan and Slave*
—	Noir Royale ground, with design as above. *Sultan and Slave*
—	Rouge Royale ground with design in both underglaze and overglaze colours depicting water lilies and bullrushes, with dragonflies in flight. *Bullrushes*
—	Vert Royale ground with design as above. *Bullrushes*
—	Rouge Royale ground with design showing a Kingfisher poised to dive from a vine stem into a pond beneath symbolised by ripples and lily leaves. Late *Kingfisher*
—	Rainbow with Garden and Bridge
—	Rouge Royale ground with fruiting vine design in gilt, with fruit in enamels. *Vine and Grape*
—	Dark blue ground with fruiting vine design in gilt, with fruit in blue enamel. *Vine and Grape*
—	Green ground with fruiting vine design in gilt, with fruit in orange, pink and green. *Vine and Grape*

Selected Bibliography

The Pottery Gazette and Glass Trade Review (Various)

English Earthenware Figures, 1740 -1940 P. A.Halfpenny

William Henry Goss and Goss Heraldic China Norman Emery (*Journal of Ceramic History*, No.4)

Price Guide to Heraldic China Nicolas Pine.

Collecting Carlton Ware published by Francis Joseph Publications.

BEVERLEY

Visit our shop with its extensive range of English and European Art Deco pottery

Monday–Thursday
11.00am–6.00pm

Friday and Saturday
9.30am–6.00pm

Sundays
By appointment

30 Church Street
Marylebone, London NW8 8EP
Tel/Fax: 0171 262 1576

Collect the Carlton Kids

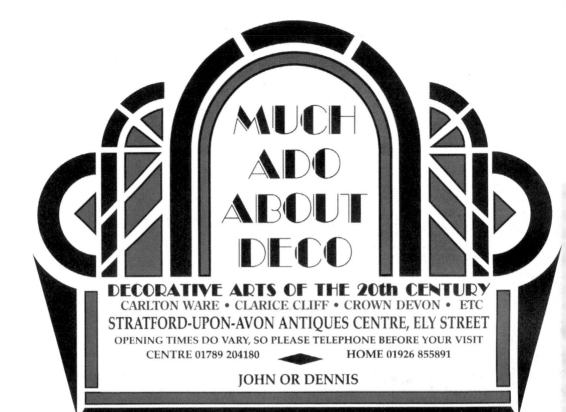